It's Not Who You Know, It's How You
TREAT THEM

Five SocialSmarts®
Secrets Today's
Business Leaders Need
to Stand Out and be
Successful

CORINNE A. GREGORY

Published by Maestrowerks, LLC.

Copyright ©2010 Maestrowerks, LLC

Printed in the United States of America

ISBN: 9780-9827981-0-2

Gregory, Corinne A.

"It's Not Who You Know, It's How You Treat Them: Five SocialSmarts® Secrets Today's Business Leaders Need to Stand Out and be Successful"

Cover Design and Layout by Dawn Teagarden

Edited by Richard Jarman

Warning: Disclaimer

To James Malinchak — From whom I learned the valuable acronym "GSDF" (Get Stuff Done Fast) as well as so many other things I take to heart,

To Craig Duswalt — Without whom this book wouldn't have "gotten done fast" — Rockstars do EVERYTHING fast! Really FAST.

To my family — Jay, Alana, Alexis, Regan — Truly you all are the source of my inspiration and for whom I do all that I do. Thanks for believing…

To my mother, Eva — Who instilled in me my earliest "SocialSmarts"

TABLE OF CONTENTS

INTRODUCTION

Have you ever wondered why some seem to have the "magic" of being able to connect with people in business, while others just seem to struggle? It truly seems sometimes as though some people "have it," while some people simply don't. And, what is "it" anyhow?

Well, the "it" is what this book is all about. "It" is the most significant differentiator businesspeople can have in today's challenging business environment. "It" has become a lost art in too many cases, something that has gone by the wayside. Truly effective leaders make powerful use of "it." You'll find it tough to become a leader these days without "it."

Our term for this powerful secret weapon? "SocialSmarts."

SocialSmarts refers to the collection of social skills, character traits and abilities you need to effectively build, nurture, and develop lasting connections with staff, employees, vendors, and customers. In today's business environment, where so much emphasis and energy is spent on individual progress and achievement, the business person who takes a different approach in his or her business dealings is certain to be noticed. This is true particularly when that approach is one that is less self-centered and self-absorbed than what appears to be the societal norm.

This book was created to share with you those SocialSmarts that you need to think, act, and be different than the rude, crude, and ego-centric mainstream. By learning and employing the Five SocialSmarts Secrets recommended in the coming chapters, you're likely to find that you'll achieve more of what you want, more easily and with less stress, and get a lot less of what you *don't* want.

But SocialSmarts isn't a one-time shot or silver bullet. You can't just put this book under your pillow and hope to absorb its lessons. So, in addition to explaining the underlying foundations and concepts you'll want to learn, I've also added some quick "takeaways" you should put into practice right away. They're called "Take 5," because they really should take you only a few minutes to put into use. They will help you immediately start seeing some changes based on action, not just theory.

I hope you benefit strongly from the information contained in this book. If you take it to heart and use the lessons and concepts presented, it will change the way you do business. It might even change your life by showing you a more inclusive, civilized way of doing things. You see, SocialSmarts aren't just for business...they're who we are and what we are, no matter what else we might be doing.

chapter One

WE DO BUSINESS WITH PEOPLE, NOT ENTITIES

The "good old days" are often spoken of as a time when life was simple and we all took care of, and respected, each other. Of course, we know that those times were somewhat exaggerated. The days of Ozzie and Harriett lifestyles were more myth than factual. However, there was a time when people assumed the best of each other and didn't require lengthy legal contracts just to "keep each other honest." Business was done on a handshake. A person's "word" was their bond.

The US Constitution, including the Bill of Rights, fits neatly on only six pages—in large letters! The document which forms the foundation on which our entire country is built, including how our government would deal with its new citizens, and how that government would be expected to run the country, took fewer pages than what today would be required for purchasing a home appliance on credit. Times have changed.

One hundred years ago, you could go to the local General Store, get what you needed for your farm, and pay for it at the end of the month, or maybe the following month. Perhaps you would trade some of your farm output to settle your bill. We all had a sense of being "in it together." We looked out for each other. Now we have become an "in it for ourselves" society.

Fast-forward to 2010. Our communiqués are flying literally at the speed of light, across vast oceans to the four points of the globe. The recipients can be in any time zone and even in places other than where we normally expect them to be. Our culture truly has become one of "business without borders," anytime, anywhere.

Yet, with whom do we usually transact that business? Not with interchangeable worker-droids, although much of today's commerce seems to be done this way. Truly effective business is still done with people we connect with. People we trust. People with whom we have developed a relationship.

Think about it: when someone we have worked with leaves one company to join another, how often do we try to find out where they went? We will often move our business dealings to maintain the business relationship with our contact. If we've developed a good bond with an individual, aren't we more likely to follow that individual to their next company, instead of simply seeking a replacement liaison at the original company? Once we've made the connection, we'd rather change companies than change the people we have grown accustomed to working with. Changing people relationships takes us out of our comfort zone. We don't know what to expect when we change the people with whom we do business.

People have been trained to be distrustful of each other. This <u>can</u> change! It starts with re-learning how to deal with people on a one-to-one basis. We may not get back to the "good old days" of the handshake contract or the running account at the General Store, but we can get back to an age of civility.

MODERN BUSINESS PRACTICES AND TECHNOLOGY CAUSES DISTANCE, NOT RELATIONSHIPS

Generally, we believe that technology has enhanced our ability to do business. As long as you consider business a "transaction"—an event or arrangement—this is probably true. We can do "transactions" all day on the Internet, through email, and using online service providers. But if we need help—to answer a question, fix a problem, confirm an action—we prefer a *person*.

Dealing with machines or nameless, faceless entities can be irritating. Which do you prefer: wading through 27 levels of company auto-attendants on their phone system, or waiting five or ten minutes to talk to an agent who can answer not only your specific question, but also any other question that may come up during the conversation? We generally feel greater comfort dealing with a person than with a machine, regardless of how fancy it may be.

Yet technology has not always been our friend when it comes to dealing with people. We've become accustomed to the anonymity of interacting with people we've never met. It's becoming harder to make and keep real connections. We rarely get the chance to learn much about the person on the other end of the keyboard, other than their email address and phone number.

It's frequently strange when we do have an opportunity to meet "for real." We don't know what to say or how to act, and the person we finally meet looks and sounds nothing like the picture we've built of them in our own heads. Once we exhaust the business issue that brought us together in the first place, we find ourselves wracking our brains for something around which to make conversation.

NETWORKING — IT'S ALL ABOUT WHO YOU KNOW

In spite of all the technology enabling our communication, we intrinsically still understand the value of personal connections. The late 1990s saw the birth and explosive growth of the concept of "networking." People made concerted efforts to attend seminars, conferences, and other events just for the purpose of trying to make connections with other people — specifically those who might be able to further their business objectives.

Technology advancements skyrocketed, which allowed us to reach out and interact with people in places we never had the ability to go before. That meant even more people were able to seek out opportunities to make connections in the hopes of forging relationships that might prove valuable now or in the future.

Often we network with a specific goal in mind: to forge a connection with Company X. While it's the company we want to build the alliance with, the reality is we need an "in." Rarely do we call the front desk at Company X, announce ourselves and say something to the effect of, "Hi, you don't know me yet, but I want to become a strategic partner of yours."

Not a very effective approach, is it? Instead, we try to find a person with whom we can connect. Through that individual, we hope to build a connection to the company. It's people-centric, not organization-centric, even if the organization is the end-goal.

PEOPLE ARE MOBILE—
YOU NEVER KNOW WHERE THEY'LL TURN UP

In 1910, people typically worked in the same place of business for the majority of their lives. The workers of today are much more mobile. A 25-year study by the U.S. Bureau of Labor Standards released in 2008 showed that today's workers change jobs every 2 1/3 years, on average. Workers in certain industries, particularly those with high-growth, may change jobs even more frequently. What this means is, for a person whose career spans 40 years or more, they may hold as many as 15-20 different jobs in their lifetime.

They may change actual careers, too, not just their jobs or companies. It's not unusual these days to hear about second- or third-career changers, people who have been downsized from one industry looking to join something different. Often, a change in life or circumstance prompts a change of interest.

There are many lessons we can take from this. For example, you must always be careful about your interactions with others. You never know where that person may end up later. Even more importantly, with the archiving abilities of email, voicemail and internet, you have to be cautious about any references in the past, too, because they may come back to haunt you. Never burn a bridge—you don't know when you might need it again.

Likewise, consider that your business relationships may have a life cycle of their own, long past the point where they seem to be immediate and relevant. If you doubt the power of prior connections, consider how popular social media sites like LinkedIn, Facebook and

Twitter have become. The first thing you do when you become a member of these sites is…you look up your friends and connections!

You usually start with your current sets of contacts, but before long you begin searching for people in your past. The sites are even offering you recommendations, based on previous job history or other connections. These may be people you haven't been in touch with for five, ten, fifteen years or more, but suddenly you're reconnected. Think about how you want them to perceive this renewed contact: will they be glad to hear from you or will they start searching for the "un-friend" or ignore button as quickly as possible?

Summary

While this first section has been brief, hopefully it has made the point that when we are "doing business" we are not interacting with nameless, faceless entities and corporations. We may be doing business with those companies, of course, but in the end, we are working with *people*. The understanding that people are vital to our business connections and, ultimately, to our outcomes, is crucial. It forms the basis for how we influence whether we have a successful or unsuccessful experience. The next chapter will begin to unlock some of those keys to success and explain why, too often, these keys today remain under-used.

Chapter Two

WHY SOCIALSMARTS®
FOR SUCCESS?

In the previous chapter, we made the case that when it comes to business, although we are working within the context of companies and organizations, we are really dealing with people — people we talk to, email, and communicate with. People we must work with, for, or alongside on a continual basis. As we become increasingly technology-dependent, our abilities to work effectively with others are becoming diminished.

Who needs "people skills" when we type one-dimensional words from a keyboard into a document, press "Send," and the recipient gets it at some unpredictable time, based on their schedule generally, not yours? Their response is likely to come back on an equally unpredictable schedule and path, but loaded with the expectation that you will respond appropriately based on their timeline, without much consideration about what's happening on your side of the dialog.

In addition, electronic "conversations" can span days rather than minutes, and any emotion of the conversation is frequently muted by the medium. Any emotion that is conveyed electronically is often misunderstood and misinterpreted. Clearly, it is easier to "not mince words" when you are not face-to-face with your counterpart. Relationships formed through email threads are difficult to build and maintain. They lack the direct, human touch, eye contact and body language.

Ah, but therein lies the key…in this world of anonymous, ambiguous and loosely defined interaction, how can anyone stand out? The answer is, you have to be smart about it—but probably not in the way you expect. Read on…

What is the Most Important Key to YOUR Success?

Since Day One of our early education, we've likely all been told to work hard, get good grades—that's the key to our success, both in school and in the work place once we leave school. But, as it turns out, it's not entirely true. Oh, sure, doing well in school is important, don't get me wrong. But it's not THE key to what makes you successful. There's something else quite a bit more important, and most people don't know it.

According to repeated studies from such well-respected academic institutions as Carnegie-Mellon University, Stanford University and the legendary Harvard University, 85% of our personal and professional success depends on our social skills. That means it's more important than our academic achievement, more important than our socio-economic background, more important than the "who we know" network. In fact, it's more important than all of those factors *combined*.

That may seem far-fetched at first, but think of it this way: don't we all know someone who is extraordinarily smart, was at the top of his or her class, is always the first one with the answer…but can't get along with others? Conversely, we also can likely identify someone who may not have had the best grades, perhaps they came from a broken home. Maybe they were dirt-poor growing up, or were abused and neglected. But, in spite of those disadvantages, they have managed to overcome them and are a real pleasure to be around, and spend time with.

Think of many of the "rags to riches" stories you know: Oprah Winfrey, Colin Powell, Walt Disney, Marshall Field, Conrad Hilton, Dave Thomas. They may not have had the best beginnings, but they were able to rise above their challenges because they were able to be comfortable around others, and to make others comfortable around them. They relied on positive character traits such as perseverance, trustworthiness, and loyalty to make their mark. In other words, they were smart in ways that matter the most: what we call *SocialSmarts*.

Not only do you know this is true from stories about successful people, but the benefit of good social skills has been studied and verified. Two recent academic studies point to how important this aspect of your development is. In October of 2008, the University of Illinois released the results of a study in which they compared two sets of high school students. Both sets were ranked equally based on their academic test scores, but one group was rated higher than the other on their social skills and interpersonal abilities.

Ten years later, the group of students that had been identified to be more socially capable, conscientious and cooperative were shown to be earning significantly more than the first group, which had similar test scores but lesser social skills.

On the heels of that report, in December, 2008, the University of Washington issued their findings of a 15-year study in which they followed a group of students who received what researchers termed, "early childhood intervention" in social skills education. They tracked these students over the course of their lives, and 15 years later, these young people were found to have better mental health, higher academic development, and better economic achievement than students who did not receive social skills training.

So, the takeaway is that not only are social skills more important than academic achievement, having these valuable skills makes success easier and better, in every area of life, including academics.

The Business Impact of Poor Social Skills

But, you say, we're all out of school at this point. Do "socialization" and social skills matter in business? Well, yes, very much so, as it turns out.

Whether you call it social skills, soft skills, people skills, interpersonal skills — whatever the phrase of the moment is — too many people lack them these days. The website BusinessDictionary.com offers this definition of social skills: the "ability to communicate, persuade, and interact with other members of the society, without undue conflict or disharmony."

Essentially, what we refer to as SocialSmarts is the set of skills, attitudes and character development that enables us to interact and communicate with others in a positive, productive way. As you read that sentence, picture in your mind typical business interactions. My guess is you'll visualize many people that don't fit the image of "positive and productive."

This is one of the biggest problems in business right now, especially as the generations of workers become younger. Surveys of employers show that the #1 complaint they have of young job candidates is that they lack the "soft skills" they need to be effective and productive in the workplace.

What kinds of things are we talking about? It runs the gamut from poor communication skills — people who are unable to communicate effectively in business, regardless of the medium for that communication. It also includes spending time surfing the Web or sending personal emails from work because the employer's Internet connection is so much faster than what they have at home. It's about being rude and callous to customers and vendors because they caught you at a bad time or get on your nerves. It's the lack of ethics and integrity that allows people to make questionable business deals that are unfair in their advantage to some favored colleagues or a preferred "in crowd," or even illegal. It's about accepting kick-backs and special perks, arranging for special treatment or favors, or engaging in business practices that are exclusionary and predatory. All these things fall within the fabric of "social skills."

Integrity and business ethics in particular are a big deal these days. Stories of Enron, WorldCom, Martha Stewart's insider trading challenges, and more serve as examples for what happens when people fail to use good judgment and ethical business practices. Unfortunately, as many incidents in the press these days show, the "new integrity" means being very sorry when you are caught doing wrong–but it isn't the thing that *keeps you from doing wrong* in the first place.

Even if we discount the (relatively) extreme cases of poor business ethics, a lack of basic social skills has a potentially negative impact on business. See if this sounds familiar: you are the customer with a challenge. You pick up the phone or come to the company offering its services with which you need help.

Even though you are the one having a problem with the company's service or product, and you are reaching out for that help, you realize within 20 nanoseconds of the phone being answered or your appearance at the "service" counter that you have seriously impinged on that employee's personal time or messed with their groove.

Whether it's the inflection of the voice on the phone or the body language when you deal with the employee in person, it's clear you are an intrusion. "Customer service" is becoming an oxymoron like "jumbo shrimp" or "government efficiency." It's enough to make you want to apologize for needing assistance, and *it's their product or service that isn't working*!

That kind of treatment can cost you customers. And lost customers are a double-problem because not only are you losing immediate revenue, you are risking your reputation in the market. I know of one company whose "sales method" was to badger its customers—not-for-profit organizations and charities—into signing questionable, obscure, long-term contracts for their services. Then, they provided shabby products and terrible customer support. When the customers tired of the poor service and unreliable products, and wanted out of the contracts, the company threatened to sue them.

How long do you think the charities would stand for this kind of treatment? What kind of reputation do you think the service provider developed in the industry? Word gets around quickly when you abuse your customers. As a result, the company's market share plummeted. It was ultimately purchased and forced to change its name in the hopes of rebuilding its dwindling business. But a change in name, without a change in policy, isn't likely to fix bad business practices.

GOOD SOCIAL SKILLS ARE A LOST ART

It's a sad commentary on our society that we can't get through a day without having someone treat us poorly, be rude, crude or disrespectful, or just plain indifferent towards us. It happens in business, it happens on our streets and in our neighborhoods. And it's getting worse.

There are many reasons for why this decline in civility and decency has come to this point; covering all the reasons why is beyond the scope of this book. (It would warrant an entire book on its own!) But we can take a look at some of the contributors in order to understand why this is such a common problem today.

First, the way we were taught good social skills — manners and character — changed dramatically about 40-50 years ago. When many of the young people of the 60s generation decided to turn their backs on what their parents, grandparents and previous generations believed in and stood for, it represented a significant shift in what was considered proper and decent behavior.

Consideration of other people's feelings and needs, or what was right and just, gave way to "if it feels good, do it." We made a transition from what's good for "us" to what's good for "me." With the transition came an increasing attitude that the end justifies the means and that if it works for me, it should be ok for you.

This attitude begins early. A 2002 survey of 12,000 high school students by the Josephson Institute showed that:

- 74% admitted cheating on an exam at least once in the past year
- 38% admitted having shoplifted at least once in the past year
- 37% admitted that they would lie "in order to get a good job"

Many of our young people today feel they don't need to deal with other people: if someone says something you don't like, you can humiliate them and assassinate their character in 27 different ways, via the Internet, cell phones and text messages, or just turn off the power switch rather than reach a resolution.

Also, as modern parents have been overly focused on building their young children's "self-esteem," they have often completely overlooked the need to develop the skill for getting along. The practice of giving every child a trophy merely for showing up as a member of a team sport is not a good paradigm for what it's like in the real world.

Not everyone has the ability to be a "super-star" on every level, but our kids have been conditioned to believe that the sun rises and sets by them. As these younger generations with their over-inflated egos and lack of effective interpersonal skills leave their homes and schools and enter the workplace, is it any wonder that there is disharmony and lack of cohesion in business?

Truly, we are reaping what we sow. The question we have to ask is: how is this helping or hurting our ability to do business? And, what type of business person and leader do you want to be: one that blends in with the crowd of self-centered, abrupt and self-serving individuals, or one who stands out by being different, using positive social skills as a powerful tool?

SUMMARY

This chapter was dedicated to the idea that the key to succeeding—in business as well as in life—depends on your abilities to successfully interact with other people. Our relationships with *people* are truly what determine success, not transactions with companies or organizations. While we may be working within the scope of the organization, we are actually working with *individuals*—individuals that have needs, desires, and goals of their own.

Our ability to make these interactions successful, to have them grow and develop beyond a superficial level, depends on our use of effective social skills—what we call SocialSmarts. It is clear from all the research presented, as well as anecdotal evidence, that social skills are a hugely critical factor in our personal and professional success. However, it is also true that positive social skills are becoming rarer in a culture that is increasingly abrupt, rude, and indifferent to the feelings and needs of others.

While it is true that acquiring and practicing positive social skills and developing good character is something ideally started early in a child's life, the good news is that it's never too late. The mission of this book is to help you acquire or hone those skills that you'll need to stand out in a positive way so you can make and grow those relationships that will really make a difference in your life, on all levels.

Now that I've made the point of how important these types of "smarts" are, in the next chapter we'll begin to dig down into the specifics of what kind of "smarts" we are talking about, and how you go about incorporating them into your business toolkit.

Take ⏳ Five

In this chapter, we offer a unique idea, one that begins to put into practice those concepts covered in the chapter. The idea is to do something, take action, in a small way that makes the concepts real and practical. Our suggestions shouldn't take long—five minutes or less. But they'll be powerful tools as you begin to develop your SocialSmarts and can start making a difference right away.

- ☐ Make a list of 10 incidents you've experienced lately where someone treated you rudely, with disrespect or indifference. Think about how that makes you feel.

- ☐ Now, make a list of 10 incidents where you were treated respectfully, where you were made to feel you were valued, particularly as a customer. My guess is this list will be harder. How does that make you feel this time?

- ☐ If you had to do business with a company whose product or service cost 10% more, but you were treated better, would you prefer that business over one that cost less but offered minimal or poor support? Consider what airline you might want to fly as a business traveler: one that offered you an extra service, like a decent hot meal or waived your luggage charge, even if it cost you $10 more for the ticket or a "no-frills" airline where you felt like cargo?

Chapter Three

SECRET #1:

IT'S ALL ABOUT ATTITUDE: HARNESSING THE POWER OF RESPECT

It may come as a surprise to you, but the biggest obstacle you face in your quest to become successful in this marketplace is you! As the incredibly successful marketeer and speaking phenomenon James Malinchak, recently shared with me, "You are six inches away from getting to where you want to be and fulfilling your dream." Any guess what those six inches represent? The space between your ears.

Truly, if you want to stand out and be noticed, you must start first with changing your mindset. It's too easy to get sucked into the idea that business is a zero-sum game, where you have to fight tooth and claw to get ahead. This is what we've been seeing for decades, and it's become second-nature. The mentality is, "In order for ME to get ahead, someone else has to get pushed aside."

The reality is, that only works for a little while. To really make headway as a business leader, you have to reset that attitude. Business, as we discussed earlier, consists of interactions between *people*, not interchangeable "carbon units." These people have feelings, wants and needs, just as valid as our own. The more adept and comfortable we become in working with those people, no matter what our position, the more we find that success is a natural result.

RESPECT—A STRATEGIC DIFFERENTIATOR

People tend to feel better about themselves when they are shown respect. Think about who you'd rather work with: someone who shows you respect and treats you like you matter, or someone who ignores you or blows by your contributions? Who do you think your customers, employees and business associates would rather do business with?

Rodney Dangerfield's hallmark complaint in the 1990s, "I get no respect," seems to be all too true. In a 2002 Gallup Poll, 80% of Americans thought lack of courtesy and respect was a serious national problem. An ABC News poll around the same time indicated 73% of Americans thought manners and behavior were worse than 20-30 years ago. You can bet that in 2010 the situation hasn't improved much, if at all.

It should not come as a big surprise then that respect can be a strategic differentiator in dealing with others in business. People in our society have become accustomed to being overlooked or dismissed by others.

When they are treated with genuine respect and consideration, it marks a refreshing change.

We are confronted daily with images and messages that remind us of our insignificance. ("Talk to the hand…," "…and this should matter to me, why?" "Clearly you're mistaking me for someone who cares.") We are virtually pre-conditioned to apologize for our need to contact or interact with others.

Here's an all-too-common scenario: you're in a meeting with a group of colleagues. There is some discussion going on about an important business matter, but several people are completely tuned out—they are busy checking their Blackberries or iPhones for messages, surfing the web, or even playing a game under the table, while the presenter talks.

Suddenly, someone asks a question of one of these individuals, but he/she is so absorbed by their own electronic activity that they miss the question entirely. When they emerge out of their text-fest and "rejoin" the meeting, the first thing they say is, "Can you repeat the question?" The message that incident sends is that the group activity is less important than the individual's activity, and the other people in the meeting—including the organizer — aren't deserving of that individual's time and attention. It's disrespectful, but we live with it every day.

What impression would it leave instead if all the participants in a meeting were actually that—participants, involved and engaged? Even if you don't have an active role in the meeting, when you give others your time and respectful attention, it sends a much different message. Meetings would likely be more productive and more effective if everyone was "on-task" instead of merely sharing space.

Further, the sense of team is much stronger if you know everyone in it is focused on the same mission.

This is not to say multi-tasking is intrinsically bad, but there is a time and a place; when you are supposed to be working with others on a specific activity, doing your own thing isn't the time or the place. It shows a lack of respect for the concerns and priorities of others.

You may remember an incident a few years ago when airline pilots flying a commercial plane filled with passengers were working on their laptops, and overshot their intended city by 150 miles. Clearly, their failure to stay on task could have been catastrophic. You may never pilot a commercial airliner, but allowing your personal needs or wishes to take over when others are depending on you in any group situation can also be a disaster — to how you are perceived.

RESPECT — THE FEELING IS MUTUAL

Operating with a respectful mindset isn't just good for the individual, it's good for the group, too. Organizations that understand how important mutual respect and personal dignity is to their workforce tend to be top performers. Take a look at *Fortune* Magazine's 2009 list of Top 100 Employers to work for. You'll see many companies in the upper ranks that are known for building a positive culture where employee contributions are valued and respected. Examples of these companies are NetApp (#1), Edward Jones (#2), Google (#4), Cisco Systems (#6), Zappos.com (#23). These companies have all managed to see increases in job growth, even in very difficult economic conditions.

If you look under the hood of these companies, you'll find a strong philosophy of believing in their workforce. They are able to make adjustments, and adapt to changing business conditions more quickly than others in their space. The truth is, organizations that are built on a foundation of respect tend to be more creative, innovative, and effective, particularly when market conditions are in flux.

When employees feel that they are treated with respect and consideration, they generally have the company's best interests at heart. This culture allows creativity to flow. Organizations that welcome out-of-the-box thinking, where there's no such thing as a dumb question, will find that the workforce feels more secure to suggest creative solutions to new challenges. They are able to make changes to processes and policies much more quickly than others in the marketplace, especially those who adhere to more traditional ideas of leaders and staff.

Zappos.com, a subsidiary of Amazon.com, is legendary for its culture of respect and creativity. When building his rapidly growing company, CEO Tony Hsieh sought the input of his employees about what they would want in a company's core values. This has resulted in a culture built on fairness, respect and humility on all levels.

The philosophy of the company allows employees to make independent decisions about how to handle customer concerns and issues, trusting its staff members to make good decisions that are in keeping with overall company practices. Zappos has seen amazing job growth in the years since it was formed, at a time where most companies were seeing significant declines.

HIGH EXPECTATIONS YIELD HIGH REWARDS

It's true that the culture of an organization can have a major effect on the performance of its staff. People tend to perform to the expectations others have of them. When you expect your employees to cheat you, work at less than their potential, and disappoint you, you'll likely get exactly what you expected. At the same time, if you have high expectations of your staff, treat them with respect, and trust that they will deliver high results, you will find that they rise to the expectations you set.

Business leaders who understand this correlation between expectations and results, and treat their employees as high-performing professionals, develop a more cohesive culture where everyone feels empowered to do their best on behalf of the organization.

Consider how employees of NetApp felt when the company threw out its former travel policy that was over a dozen pages long in favor of a new philosophy that said, essentially, it expected its employees to make good frugal decisions about travel while respecting their needs to be rested and appropriately accommodated. Do you think most people within NetApp will use good judgment when making travel plans since they know the company trusts in their ability to do so independently?

Many large companies have hourly employees "clock in" using a time clock, which tracks how long they are in the building, but not how long they are on the job. It creates a "them versus us" relationship between salaried employees and management, who are expected to work to accomplish their assigned tasks, and the hourly employees who are expected to show up for a finite period of time.

What role does the time clock play in evaluating the quality of their work, or their focus on their tasks? The answer: there is no automatic correlation between time in the building, and tasks accomplished. Imagine how much more mutual respect there would be if the time clocks were eliminated, and management said to their hourly employees, "We trust you to do your job well, and to be honest about how many hours you worked when filling out your time card." Yes, they still fill out a time card if they are hourly employees, but they don't need a mechanical device to verify that they are being truthful.

Expecting them to deliver an honest day's work for an honest day's wage is a sign of mutual respect. Believing in the best of your people and expecting them to deliver accordingly is also more likely to develop loyalty and support for the mission of the organization. Companies that operate this way will continue to hold that loyalty in tough times — a rare commodity in these turbulent conditions, where staff is likely to jump ship at the first sign of trouble.

Do As I DO, not Just as I Say: Leading by Positive Example

The days of ordering people around like an obnoxious drill sergeant and expecting the "minions" to do your bidding are so, *yesterday*. Sure, there are people out there who still do it, and underlings that respond, but it's not out of respect–it's out of fear (think Gordon Gekko from the movie "Wall Street"). Most people prefer to work for people who make them feel valued and respected, not the ones who love to lord their authority over the "little people." In fact, it's those "little people" who make your organization successful, or not. Studies show that employees who feel disrespected or belittled in their work environment are three times more likely to leave than those who are treated with dignity.

Think about the cost of that attrition to your company — replacement costs, learning curve, possibly even severance or out-placement programs for the exiting employee. If that employee was a valued member of the team, it may cost even more as colleagues leave, too.

Leadership by positive example means several things. It means you treat your employees at least as well as you expect to be treated. It means you give them a chance to be heard. It means you consider their opinions, even if you don't agree. If the decision is ultimately yours to make, that's fine. But, you'll get better buy-in on your decision if you at least have made an effort to involve others in dialog, and consider their viewpoint.

Treat people fairly,—and that means everyone, not just the superstars or the ones you like best. It seems obvious, but it's not always easy to put into actual practice. Some people just annoy us. We don't like dealing with them. But, take comfort in the thought that other people feel that way about us, too!

The real mark of a positive leader, however, is when you can manage to consider the other person's value to the organization and its mission, and treat them accordingly, without ever letting on that they grate on your one remaining nerve. One trick to doing this is to find one thing about that person you can respect or appreciate, and focus on that. Practice giving them a compliment about what you value in them. You may be surprised at the reaction and results — both in the employee and in yourself!

Another way leaders serve as a positive example is by sticking to the same rules and policies as the ones they expect their employees to follow. Instead of behaving as though you are above the riff-raff by virtue of your position, and are therefore entitled to special perks and treatment, consider the message it sends when you hold yourself true to fair practices. Perhaps that means you don't take extra-long lunch breaks, or come in habitually late.

For example, there are many heads of innovative and leading organizations that make it a practice of having the same size office as their staff, share meals in the same cafeteria, or turn down a fancy company car. A strong military general knows that, during a tough campaign, he must take care of the needs of his troops, before he himself gets to bed down. It may seem like a simple thing, but those actions demonstrate the concern the general has for his troops; as a result, they will follow that general willingly into battle, knowing that he cares about them.

Summary

The present marketplace has conditioned us to think that we must make other people less in order for us to appear "more." This attitude is so prevalent and pervasive that it has nearly become the rule in business. The business leader who can stand against that philosophy, and treat his or her employees, colleagues and business partners with respect and consideration is a refreshing standout.

Management by insecurity doesn't work for long. At some point, you'll find someone who is bigger, smarter, or more forceful than you who won't accept being bullied or intimidated. Learning to work *with* people and developing a true team spirit based on mutual respect is a lot easier than having to continually work around people.

Don't be like the characters in the comic strip Dilbert! They are constantly put down and belittled by their tyrant boss, — and do all they can to fulfill his low expectations as a result. If you build into your employees the mindset that they are valuable, and you expect a lot from them because you know they can do a lot, they'll rise to your level of expectation.

The culture of respect you develop is a powerful tool in overcoming challenges or adversity in your organization. People will be more willing to pull together and follow your lead if they know they can believe in you and your ability to be there for them.

Take ⏳ Five

Here are a few quick actions you can do in five minutes or less to support the idea of the Power of Respect. These actions will show how it can be a strategic differentiator in your business or dealings with others.

> Give a genuine compliment to three people on your team or with whom you do business, every day. Make it a habit.

> Offer to help someone with a task. This is particularly powerful if it's someone you don't normally work with. Think about how you can help them.

> Walk through your team's area at least once a day, and greet every member of the team with a smile. Thank them for what they do.

chapter Four

SECRET #2:

TURNING "WHAT'S IN IT FOR ME?" INTO "WHAT'S IN IT FOR US?"

Business transactions of all kinds have been focused on "gain." Gaining mindshare, gaining market, increasing profits and revenues, cornering the market, outpacing the competition. It's not necessarily a bad thing—we are all trying to grow our opportunities and outcomes. The goal of any business is to grow and prosper—you're generally in business to achieve something. The question, particularly these days, is, at what cost?

Many businesses are looking to grow at *any* cost, including short-cuts to business processes and service, undercutting the competition, and even implementing shoddy or unethical business practices. That gives _you_ a real opportunity to stand out. It's all about how you approach business and treat the connections you are trying to make with your customers, vendors or suppliers, or the public. Again, it starts with attitude, as we discussed in the previous chapter.

In this chapter, we'll show you how you use the Power of Respect to retool your business thinking so that you can be more successful, more easily when approaching potential business connections or transactions. I'll show you how to set your mindset on the most powerful way to operate and act. It will surprise people because it has both everything — and nothing — to do with YOU.

News Flash: It's NOT all about YOU

Has this ever happened to you? You attend a business or social event and you meet someone new. After the first initial greeting, your new best friend spends the next 20 minutes telling you all about him- or herself ("How do you DO that without taking a breath?" you wonder). You never get a chance to participate. The clincher is when the "conversation" is over and they finish by saying, "Well, I'm really glad I met you and got to know you. Let's do this again soon. Maybe lunch?"

Uh, no. Not likely to happen. This was not a conversation, it was a dump. A very one-sided dump. It was clear that the other person was all about "me" and didn't care much about you. That "let me tell you all about me" or "what's in it for ME" attitude is very off-putting. It's an impediment to building, keeping, and developing good, strong, mutual relationships. There's nothing mutual about that kind of approach.

Similarly ineffective is this scenario in business: Let's say you are about to do a demo of your product or service for a prospective customer. You've done this presentation a hundred times (or it may be the *first* time), and you just KNOW what you have to offer is exactly what they are looking for. So, you go through your litany of features, clicking through what you have smoothly and effortlessly... you are "in the zone."

At the end of the presentation, you look at the customer, convinced that you've sold them on what a terrific opportunity you're offering them, and say: "So, what do you think?" You are surprised when the silence is deafening on the other side. Are those crickets chirping in the background?

What went wrong? You did a great job. The value of your product or service should be obvious. Well, the problem is that you've just given your prospective customer what we lovingly call in the industry, "the bennie-barf." In other words, you've told them all about what YOU can provide, without really giving them a chance to say what they needed.

Now, the reality is you may know EXACTLY what it is they need, but that's not the point. THEY have to feel as though they are a participant in the process. They aren't going to listen to what you can offer if you haven't given them a chance to tell you what their issue is, or what specific problem it is they are trying to solve. Let's put it another way: they won't HEAR you if you don't first listen to THEM.

It may seem a little backwards, particularly if you are very good at what you do. You may think you already know the questions they are going to ask, so you're prepared and you jump on the answers. Maybe as a way of showing how well you know their business or what they need, you even try to make a connection by saying something like, "I know what you're going to say…"

Only, you really don't. Even if you know, generally, what the typical question is, you don't know *exactly* what they are going to say, unless you truly are clairvoyant. You are being presumptuous if you tell them you know what they are going to say, know what they need, or know what they are looking for. You come off as a know-it-all. It's hard for people to connect with that kind of person.

Consider this from the other person's standpoint. Who is the primary "actor" in the previous scenario? It's all about YOU, isn't it? Because you have the "solution," you must already be light-years ahead of their problem. It's about what you can sell them, not how you can help them. And, while that seems like a subtle nuance, it's really a huge distinction. It may make all the difference in the world between making and keeping those winning connections, and being just another one of those "typical" business people who are always pushing their stuff on others.

Let's take an alternate approach, and consider which you would prefer, if you were the customer. At the beginning of your pitch or meeting, what if you began with something like, "I have a great deal of valuable information about our product or service to share with you, but before we get started, I'd like to make sure we cover YOUR specific issues. Is there any burning question you'd like to get answered right now? Is there something you need to have addressed in the course of our discussion that would make it worthwhile for you?"

Notice how you have put the emphasis on THEM? Solving their problems, answering their questions? It's not about you…it's about how you can address their needs. At the very beginning of the dialog, you've made it clear your job is to serve <u>their</u> needs, which means it's worth <u>their</u> time to listen to you. By putting yourself in the position of serving them, you've already made major progress in overcoming their reluctance to accept what it is you're "selling."

Why is this important? Well, for one, people have a natural tendency to resist being sold to. And when I say "sold," I don't mean only in the strictly literal sense. It can mean offering a service that really benefits the customer, but comes at a higher cost than what was budgeted (even if it is the only logical choice.) It can be trying to form an alliance with someone else, or asking for an introduction to someone influential, or even asking for a recommendation.

"Selling" is any activity or communication that involves you persuading another person to do something you want them to do. If the action you want them to take is not the other person's own idea and initiative, it's "selling," regardless of what the action is. Even "marketing" is "selling" — it's just approaching the sale in a different way, geared toward trying to get people to want what it is you have, without your having to push it to them.

Most people have a natural "repel" instinct when it comes to being sold something. And, if you come in with an attitude of "I'm here to help you," the first reaction you'll likely get is, "Uh, I didn't need your help." Just reframing this approach to a "how can I help *you*?" or "what is the problem *you* are trying to solve?" takes the emphasis off you, and places the focus on the other party.

But you have to be genuine. The other real turnoff in the business world is the person who is trying to "suck up" to you, or appears to be your oldest and dearest buddy in an attempt to slide into that relationship. Combine "fear of selling" with "aversion to suck ups" and you've lost your ground entirely.

Put yourself authentically in the position of your customer or business partner, saying, "What problem/challenge are you trying to solve?" Truly listen to the answer given. Then respond (again, genuinely) with "Let's see how I/we can help you with that." These steps will take you much farther than the best "bennie barf" or "suck up" you've ever tried!

You're making it clear that you are all about them, you're really here to help, and you're not just about making the sale. In this world of high competition and "me too" products and services, your customer can always get another widget, another car, another doctor or dentist, another attorney right around the corner. It's the connection with *you* — the person who knows and understands their issues and is actually there to help — that will make the difference between whether they choose your widget, or go elsewhere.

Co-Powerment®

Surely we've all heard about the concept of "Empowerment." Merriam-Webster's Dictionary defines empowerment as: "to enable. To promote the self-actualization or influence of." It's a popular topic: Do a quick search on Amazon.com, for example, and you'll get nearly 5000 results—for *books alone*. Here are some sample titles:

+ "Empowerment: The Art of Creating Your Life as You Want It"

+ "Empowerment: You Can Do, Be, and Have All Things!"
+ "Ten Steps to Empowerment"

- "The Women's Book of Empowerment"
- "The Three Keys to Self-Empowerment'

Here's a great one: "Self-Empowerment 101: Re-enchantment with our own capacity for empowering ourselves and others."

Or, a variation of the "Empowerment" theme: "The Six Keys to Unlock and Empower Your Mind: Spot Liars & Cheats, Negotiate Any Deal to Your Advantage, Win at the Office, Influence Friends, & Much More."

Can you spot the common thread here? It's not easy to miss. It's all about "me." Empowering Me, making myself more, self-actualization and self-realization…it's about "unlocking the power"…within ME. There are "Empowerment" seminars—for men, for women, for athletes—Youth Empowerment, Empowerment Therapy, "Maximum Success Empowerment," and in case the emphasis on "me" wasn't enough, there are even "self-empowerment seminars." There are more than 179,000 results returned in a simple Google search of "empowerment seminars."

This is all well and good. We should feel strong and "empowered" to do what we are meant to do. Being able to tap into and make the most of our potential, abilities and energy is great—too many people underestimate their own capabilities. But the topic of "empowerment" has become so self-focused and me-centric that it leaves little room for all the other "empowered" people with whom we need to interact and get along.

Unless you are an "idealist" entrepreneur, a truly sole proprietor (but even then you're not doing business "alone"), or a hermit, your success depends in some degree on other people. Those other people have needs, goals, requirements, business objectives and so forth, just like you do. It seems obvious, but it's easy to lose sight of this in business, when the job we need to do naturally gets the bulk of our attention. It can be frustrating when we find ourselves in situations where other people don't seem to find our needs quite so important or urgent.

There's also the issue of what some people refer to as "personal baggage" — things not directly business-related that affect how people operate, respond, or react in the business environment. Some examples are health issues, personal or family situations, the weather — truly any of a hundred things that can affect a person. All these things can color the working environment or working relationships. They are factors that must also be taken into account.

It's a reality: we depend on others to get "stuff" done in the workplace. We can't do it all ourselves, or at least, not for long. It makes sense, then, that all the "empowerment" in the world isn't going to amount to much if we can't find a way to exist and operate cohesively with those others on whom we depend.

While you might think of this mutual dependency as being "co-dependent" in the purest sense, that word won't work; we needed another word to describe the type of working relationship that is able to leverage the distinct power of individuals, but in a way that also taps into the power of the group. We call that term, "CoPowerment," which is the art and skill of turning "me" into "we." Another way to think of it is evolving from asking, "What's in it for ME?" to asking, "What's in it for US?"

If this is a little fuzzy to you, here's an example of what I mean, from the 1982 blockbuster movie _Star Trek: The Wrath of Khan_. It's the spectacular scene where First Officer Spock is dying, having sacrificed himself to save the rest of the crew of the Enterprise. Captain Kirk is devastated at Spock's heroic act, which has cost Kirk's friend his life. Spock explains his actions by pointing out that the "needs of the many outweigh the needs of the few…or the one."

No, I'm not suggesting we follow in Spock's path and sacrifice ourselves or our needs exclusively to support the "greater good." Some people might interpret Spock's comment as call for a socialist way of life. This is not meant to be an endorsement or even a suggestion of a socialistic approach, or even the "it takes a village" mentality. Regardless of whether it _takes_ a village or not, most of us do at least live and work in places where other people are. We have to accept the idea of shared and mutual goals in order to be effective in that environment.

What this means in a business context may change how you view your role. Truly, you may think that your job is to be "the boss," the driving force, or the one who makes things happen. That may be true, to some extent. But, it's how you go about implementing that role that gives you a greater or lesser opportunity for stand-out success.

I challenge you to think of it this way: your job as a leader is to help clear a path that allows your team to do what you hired them to do. Your team doesn't have to be all internal employees, either. You can include outside vendors, suppliers, business colleagues or partners in that definition with equal validity.

Certainly, the concept of enabling your team to do their job isn't new or revolutionary. One term used to describe that sort of approach is "Servant Leadership," but that implies that someone has to *lower* themselves to be of service to others. Again, our egos tend to have trouble with that idea.

We believe CoPowerment is a better description of what occurs in truly engaged and effective teams. This term recognizes that everyone is invested in a shared, successful end-goal, which results in group, and individual, success. Your role as a wise, successful leader is to leverage your skills, along with those of your team members, to develop the culture of respect and mutually shared goals that allows the success "magic" to occur.

FIND THE MUTUAL "WIN"

Throughout history, we've been conditioned to know that the normal outcome of any conflict is a "win-lose" scenario—one person wins, the other one loses. You can't have a winner without an at-least equal and opposite "loser." Too often, doing business was a lot like "conflict resolution," in that you had to "win" in order to make a sale, form an alliance, or deliver a product.

The problem with that early "win-lose" scenario is that it implied in order for you to win, the other party involved had to "lose." Not very positive, particularly in sales and customer service. Think about it: if you "win" the sale, does it mean the victim…er, *customer*… has to "lose?" Lose what? Money? Resistance? It was a classic competitive style. And, as we all know, business *is* competitive.

But a "win-lose" scenario sounded so harsh and predatory. So, in the early 1980s, a new phrase was born, again stemming from conflict resolution models. The "win-win" scenario implied a much more even-handed approach, one where both sides sought to benefit from a proposed transaction. "Win-win" was adopted by so many different sales and business philosophies that it practically became a religion, a much-chanted mantra for success.

While it may seem that "win-win" is somehow a collaborative or inclusive style of conducting business, it really isn't. It's only a two-sided transaction, which really misses the point of true collaboration: creating something together that's bigger and better than what we can accomplish individually.

Hence, a new philosophy—find the mutual win, or what I'm calling the "win-win-win." What this means is, find that point where you can determine what the good is for you (increased sales, higher visibility, increased product/service awareness), what the good is for the other party (a new distribution channel, access to desired product/service) and then determine how both sides might benefit *jointly* from the offer.

There is an old saying that God gave us two ears and one tongue, but not the wisdom to use them in their proper proportion. In the old school of sales, it used to be said that "Once you ask a closing question, the first person who speaks loses." We no longer want a win/lose relationship as previously discussed, so this philosophy no longer holds. However, it does make sense to get your customer/prospect talking, and keep him/her talking. The more they talk, the more you learn, and that is the objective. When you learn what they want and need, you can easily match their needs with what you have to offer. Remember, two ears, one tongue, used in that proportion!

In a "win-win-win" scenario there is true collaboration. Both sides are looking not only for what works for each individual party, but what can be developed out of the collaboration or partnership. Referrals are a very common form of this type of arrangement. Perhaps Business A doesn't have the specific product, service or expertise needed by a client. But, as part of a referral program with Business B (who CAN fulfill the client's needs), Business A ends up with a happy client who receives the service they need from Business B. This can also lead to a strategic partnership between Business A and Business B, a revenue-share model that is based on mutual business transactions.

But, it takes people to make these things happen! It takes people who feel that making connections and opening up channels with other like-minded individuals makes more sense than trying to control the opportunity themselves. It has to be done from a genuine sense of "partnership" rather than a sense of "we gotta get more business." Otherwise, the wrong underlying attitude comes through.

What do I mean, specifically? Well, if you approach a new initiative with a key person at Business B (we'll call them BusinessRep B) with the attitude of "what's in it for ME?" then you've already come with the wrong mindset. You're approaching BusinessRep B with a sales mentality. You're already telegraphing: "What can an alliance with THEM do for me? I'll have to convince them that it's a good thing." You'll end up wasting a lot of time trying to talk BusinessRep B into wanting to do business with you.

Also, keep in mind that the less connected you are with BusinessRep B at the outset, the more convincing you'll have to do. As we discussed earlier, when people are being sold to, their natural inclination is to resist. Hence the classic term, "overcoming the *obstacles* to 'yes.'"

Now, consider this alternative approach. Do your homework first. Put yourself in the place of BusinessRep B — why would he/she want to enter into such a business arrangement with you? There is a simple way you can do this: ask BusinessRep B (either actually or virtually) "How can I help YOU?" By putting yourself in a position of service to BusinessRep B, you do several things:

1. You reset your thinking to consider what's in it for THEM first

2. You are already telegraphing the attitude that you understand it's not about you and what you can get from the arrangement

3. By approaching it from what Business B (or BusinessRep B) has to gain, you're more than ½ way to overcoming obstacles, because you answer the questions before they are even asked.

Put yourself in the other person's shoes. Would YOU prefer to be approached by:

- Someone who you can tell is looking for their own strategic edge but is cloaking their real motives in a veil of "hey, this'll be good for both of us!"

- Or, by someone who clearly has considered already what the benefits are to you and is offering you an opportunity to get involved?

Likely the latter. Lead with an offer first. You will find it's a lot easier to "sell" to someone who *wants* what you have, rather than trying to convince them to buy.

Now, finally, the last part—the "what's in it for all of US?" we started this discussion with. Again, you'll be much better positioned to know that answer if you've done your homework from Business

B's perspective than if you approach them cold hoping they'll see the "synergy."

Why would a collaborative arrangement be good for you both? Would it open up new channels that weren't previously there? Is there a way to leverage each other's business contacts? Can you, together, create a market offering that wouldn't be there without your connection? Aristotle was right when he said that "the whole is greater than the sum of its parts." That's exactly what CoPowerment is all about.

Consider the following: A family wants to go to the mall for some shopping on Saturday. But, there are many household chores to be done. Dad and Mom gather the kids and ask, "Who wants to go to the mall?" All answer in the affirmative, so a deal is struck. The kids get the kitchen in order, and do the vacuuming. Dad and mom get the yard work done in record time.

All chores completed, the family heads off to the mall, with most of the day remaining for shopping and maybe a movie. Without all family members pitching in, the day would be lost to the chores, and no mall activity would be in play. The kids found their "win" by helping do something they might not want to do, and mom and dad got help so they would not have to do all the work themselves. The sum of the total (an entire family enjoying an afternoon at the mall) was greater than the individual activities each could have done on their own.

So it can be if we think, "What's in it for US?" All of us. It's an outward-thinking focus that can work for everyone involved.

Summary

In this chapter, we covered the idea that it's your overall attitude and approach that will have the biggest impact on your business effectiveness. If you follow the traditional and typical philosophy that business is a "win-lose" or even a "win-win" proposition, you're already placing yourself at a disadvantage. The key to building and maintaining successful, long-lasting relationships lies in utilizing the power in a true collaborative relationship, one in which everyone is both individually a winner, in addition to reaping the benefits of building a bigger "win" together.

If you take to heart the attitude of "What's in it for us?" you'll find that your business dealings go much easier and more smoothly. But, it's *imperative* that you are genuine about this. Nobody likes a phony, and the only thing worse than a phony is a phony who is trying to sell you or talk you into doing something.

The true collaborative nature, — of turning "what's in it for ME," into "what's in it for US" — is what we have termed CoPowerment. It is a strategically different way to do business. Truly CoPowered business transactions and ventures will be the most effective. They will endure, because all sides are committed to finding and developing those processes and end-products that last. Further, the people at the core of those transactions are motivated and inspired by shared philosophies, instead of those that are one-sided or predatory.

Take ⏳ Five

Here are a few quick actions you can do in five minutes or less to support the idea of finding a mutual "win" and reframing "What's in it for ME?" to "What's in it for US?"

☐ When engaged in a conversation, try counting silently to three before responding to what you just heard. Take a moment to take it all in.

☐ Instead of starting a conversation or presentation with your goals, turn the focus around to the other party and ask them what they would like to achieve or gain from the event. Make it clear your interest is in serving their needs.

☐ Each day, ask someone on your team — whether internal or extended — what you could do to help them today. There may be nothing they need from you at this time, but the fact that you have taken time to check in with them will speak volumes about your concerns for their ability to do their job. Be sincere when you ask, and focus on their answer — don't make your response seem automatic or superficial. Be sure you follow through if you commit to taking an action.

Chapter Five

SECRET #3:

PERCEPTION IS REALITY: MAKING A WINNING FIRST IMPRESSION

YOUR FIRST IMPRESSION: IT HAPPENS FASTER THAN YOU THINK

Have you ever heard this phrase: "You never get a second chance to make a first impression?" Not only is that true, but my guess is you don't realize how quickly that first impression is set. How long do you think it takes someone's brain, on average, to lock in that impression upon meeting a person for the first time? I like asking that question when I do my presentations. The answers I get from the audience vary from one second to five minutes or more.

The real answer: 27 seconds.

To appreciate how little time that really is, I encourage you to take a look at your watch–if it has a seconds hand–and count off 27 seconds. I do this when speaking in front of business groups. I've even done this with my youth groups or school-based presentations. It makes the point. It's not much time at all. It's about enough time to approach someone, get within "social distance," stick out your hand, shake hands, and make about one comment per side. Done.

Since you only have 27 seconds, you'd better make the best use of it. The corollary to my quote in the previous paragraph is that while it only takes a few seconds to make that first impression, it takes much longer than that to reset or correct a less-than-stellar impression, if you can at all. Careers can be made or broken based on what happens in that sub-minute interval. You want to be sure you are using that time to present yourself in the best possible manner.

In the business world, there are expectations for how we behave when we meet someone. In general, as I just described above, we make our approach, shake hands, introduce ourselves if necessary, make eye contact when speaking, then progress to the next logical step. That step might be to make light business or casual chat, or to move to a meeting room. Ideally, all this is done smoothly and with great confidence–but that's often where things get challenging.

The handshake—let's examine that for a minute. What constitutes a "good" handshake? It should be firm, but not bone-crushing—it's not an arm-wrestling match. The "alpha" doesn't prove him/herself by the handshake.

Likewise, beware of what I call the "dead fish." Oh, we've all had this one…the person with whom you're shaking hands gives you this limp, sometimes slightly-damp paw to barely grasp; as soon as you touch palms you're tempted to check for a pulse. There is no nice way of putting this: it's icky. I shook hands with a very famous actor once several years ago. He was known for his virility and manliness. But I got a dead fish from him. To this day, it has altered my impression of him. That's how powerful a mere handshake can be.

A good handshake is simple to make: just aim for what I call "web-to-web" contact. Make sure the web of skin between your thumb and index finger meets the web of the other person's hand. Wrap your fingers around the other person's hand in a natural way and squeeze moderately. That's it. "Shake" by pumping your arm, from the elbow, about 2-4 times; less is dismissive and weird, more and it seems like you're getting overly friendly or enthusiastic. It's a simple thing, really, but one that packs a lot of message in a non-verbal way.

Another huge part of meeting people is eye contact and speaking *to* the other person. Again, it sounds simple, but so many people have trouble making eye contact. I'm not suggesting you stare fixedly into the other person's eyes—that would give anyone but a sociopath the creeps. But look in the general direction of your listener's eyes when you speak to them.

Here's a trick, if you can't feel comfortable making continued eye contact: when you first start speaking, look the person in the eyes. Then, you can move your focus slightly away from their eyes—perhaps to their nose or slightly to one side of their nose or the other. When you get ready to finish speaking, return your focus to their eyes.

If you doubt the power of following appropriate cultural expectations for interpersonal communication and first impressions, let me pose a scenario. Imagine you are a hiring manager in a US-based business. You have two equally-qualified candidates to interview—one from the mainstream US culture and another one from, say, a Hispanic culture.

In many cultures, children are taught that to be properly respectful to an authority figure, you show them by your conduct—your voice, your body language, how you address them—that you are submissive to them. That's polite in a Latin culture.

Now imagine you're doing the first "meet and greet" with your two candidates. The mainstream candidate comes to you with a firm handshake, makes eye contact, and connects well with words and actions upon meeting you. The second candidate does what is culturally appropriate for him or her: lessens their hand pressure against yours in the handshake, looks away from you when you speak, and withdraws their posture or "lowers" themselves in recognition of your authority.

Regardless of their abilities, who made the stronger first impression? Who do you think you're most likely to hire? Most likely the mainstream candidate.

It's not racism or cultural snobbery that's going on. We tend to relate better to people who conform to our expectations. That confident first impression is the one most likely to instill confidence in us. Now, once we're past that point, we may find that there are other things that favor one person over another. But those first 27 seconds go a long way toward forming a picture in our minds of *who* that other person is and *what* they are. Remember that the next time you go to meet someone for the first time. Make sure those 27 seconds are used not just the right way, but the best way.

We DO Judge a Book by its Cover

It's another old adage: you can't judge a book by its cover. But it's simply not true. While perhaps we shouldn't judge books by their cover, we really do. We judge people the same way. Whether we mean to or not, our brains form impressions of other people based on a number of different factors. How they dress, the condition of their hair, the expression on their face, how they hold their bodies, how they speak — all these things go into our assessment of the whole "package."

Let's examine the book metaphor for a minute, and see how psychology works. Imagine for a minute that you are in a bookstore. You're looking for something new to read, but you have no specific title in mind. You wander the shelves, heading to your favorite genre. The first thing that attracts you to a particular book is…the cover. Does the outside "look" get your attention? In other words, is the cover appealing? Colors, layout of elements, even the typestyle of the title all go into designing an appealing cover.

If this cover works for you, the next step is typically to turn to the back cover — dig a little deeper. What does the author offer on the back? A brief description of the contents, a tease of what the book is about, or something about the author's background. The back pieces must reinforce or augment what the expectations of the cover set up for you. Otherwise, you're likely to just put it back on the shelf.

Now, if you're sold on the spot, great! But if you're still not sure, you might crack open the book at the beginning, or some random spot in the book to check it out a little further. Then, another decision point: buy or put back?

That's very similar to the assessments our brains make when we meet someone for the first time. Our "cover" is our outward appearance. It's how we dress, how we've "put ourselves together," even sometimes the *colors* we choose to wear that have a significant impact on "buy or put back" decision others make about us.

Most of us, when we get ready for business or work in the morning, think about what <u>we</u> want to wear that day. But I want to offer a different perspective: to make the best impression, you have to consider factors beyond yourself. Ask yourself, what do I think other people are expecting me to look like? How do I dress this morning in a way that supports (or sometimes *redirects*) that image? At this point you might be thinking, "What?!!?" Let me explain—and in the interest of full disclosure, this isn't just a "woman" thing.

I often consider the psychology of my "packaging" when I am meeting someone or speaking to a group for the first time. Maybe I'm personally feeling very strong and confident that day, so I'm inclined to wear a strong color—maybe even a red blazer. But, I realize that given the person I'm meeting, why I'm meeting them and the role that they have, wearing "power colors" such as red or orange might be a bit off-putting or intimidating (yes, someone who's 5' 3" and has a fighting weight of 100 lbs soaking wet can still be intimidating!). So, I elect to wear something a little more subdued.

Other times, I may not be feeling quite as spunky. But, I need to project a strong image, so I may choose to wear a stronger color or cut of an outfit, in order to mesh with the expectations of the people I'm meeting. When I'm working with kids or speaking to youth groups, I tend to go trendier in my choice of outfits because that's necessary for the kids to relate to me. It doesn't mean I am being less "me," or that I'm manipulating my audience. It means I am sensitive to their expectations of the "cover" they're going to see once they've selected me off the shelf, as it were.

Think of it this way: put yourself in the place of the person or group you are meeting and evaluate yourself. Consider what they will see when they are looking at you. Is this the impression you want them to have?

Now we've passed the cover stage. Keep this in mind: everything else about us from here on out can either support and reinforce that first impression, or negate it. For example, you may be dressed well and appropriately. But if your speech is riddled with "um" and "uh" or "yeah, man," what impression will that leave? I'm not saying it's right or wrong—things are largely "right or wrong" based on situation, time and place. But be aware of those elements of your package. Be conscious about your choices. When I'm working with kids or youth, I may be more energetic, and my speech may be more relaxed and loose But I don't speak that way in a national radio interview!

Here's another thing to be conscious of: your overall demeanor. Perhaps you are naturally energetic. You must let that energy out, or you feel you're going to explode. Maybe you are a toe-wagger, pencil-tapper, finger-drummer, or knuckle-cracker. I understand; I fidget myself. You need to realize, though, that to someone looking at you who may not know about your energetic tendencies, it might come across as impatience or boredom. This is particularly true if you're not focused on the other person or what's going on in the group.

I was given this piece of advice once that I'll pass on to you: no matter where you are or what you are doing, assume that someone is watching you. The more people in a group, the more likely it is that someone has you in their sight at any given moment. No, this is not meant for you to be narcissistic, or figure that you're such a big deal that people naturally flock to you. It's the law of averages coupled with Murphy's Law. Meaning, in this case, the more unflattering a moment you are having, the more you can be assured someone is seeing it happen!

Think of the times you have seen politicians or celebrities caught in "awkward" moments. They are hard to miss, because these moments get re-broadcast on YouTube and on all the cable channel shows: TMZ, Extra, ET, and so on. Of course, the awkward moment was captured because as a celebrity or politician, there is always a camera lurking nearby. Fully aware of the cameras, they still got caught saying something or doing something they would have rather had gone unnoticed.

The next time you are in a group, imagine that someone, anyone, or everyone has a camera to catch your every move. Would you let that "itch" scratch itself, think twice before adjusting your clothing, or hold fire on that slightly off color quip? Probably so. It takes only one misstep to undue lots of good. The Navy has an expression: "Loose lips sink ships," which was created to underscore that you never know who you are talking to. It may even be a person who has a reason to harm you. Don't be sunk by your own torpedo.

The basic message here is this: just like a book, you want to make sure your "cover" represents the way you want people to see you. Once you've gotten past that stage, your words and initial behaviors represent the "back cover." Again, the people you are meeting are making a decision: does this person meet our expectations? If so, you pass on to the next stage, which allows people to get to know you, your abilities, and your capabilities a little further.

All along the way you have "pass or fail" checkpoints. As long as the approval light remains "green," people will continue to accept you, do business with you, and want to deepen the relationship. To continue the book analogy, most of the time people will know what they think they need to know within the first chapter or two. Do what you can to continue their desire to get that far and you'll be just fine.

It's all About Connections

Ha! At this point you're probably thinking: "See, she IS going to tell me it's about who I know, after all." Those aren't the kind of connections I'm going to talk about, sorry. Yes, "who you know" can be very important. But if you can't connect with those "Whos," it doesn't much matter. You can't form relationships based just an introduction or chance meeting. Where do you go from there, when you want to turn a one-time encounter into a friendship, business relationship, alliance, or all of the above?

It's about connecting. One-on-one.

So you're past the first impression stage. Now we're into "what's next." As a general rule, when you are communicating with another person, they have an expectation that you are engaged and focused.

What does that mean exactly? To put it simply: they want your attention, regardless of the communication medium or situation.

Let's look at a couple of situations and examine "connectedness" in each:

In-person meeting

When you are face-to-face with someone, be exactly that—face-to-face. That means making eye contact during discussions, speaking *to* them and *with* them, not gazing off in the distance like you're looking for someone better to come along. It means being focused on your conversation and staying engaged with the topic, not interrupting, or allowing your thoughts to drift.

It can be tough sometimes, but it's important to stay "present" in the situation. It's true that we all find ourselves going on tangents or drifting off in our minds on occasion, again consider the impression it leaves on the person or people around you. But consider the message you send when you are bored, self-absorbed, or could care less about what's going on. As a teacher once told me, "If you aren't really interested, at least have the class to *fake* it."

And if you have to fake it all the time or most of the time, ask yourself honestly: "Why are you here at all?"

On the Phone

This can sometimes be even harder than face-to-face meetings. There are so many things that can compete for our attention when we don't have "full focus," using all our faculties. Communication can be more difficult too, each time you remove a layer of "personal connectedness."

In a face-to-face situation, what you say can be supported by action or even by body language. You have the full five senses to work with. On the phone (with the exception of tele-video conferencing or facilities like Skype), you've already lost one layer — visual. So you have to rely on tone and words to show attention, interest and connection. As I said, it's easier to drift off the conversation because your "visual" can get derailed by something else that captures your attention: your cell phone, someone walking by your office, a report, a magazine article, or an email alert that pops up on a computer screen.

Try to stay in the moment as much as possible. Focus on the caller. Pay particular attention to differences between the other person taking a breath, and finishing a sentence. Otherwise, you may find yourself inadvertently interrupting. This can be particularly challenging with cell phones because the fidelity isn't always as good as it is on a landline. Plus, there is often a slight delay, so you may find yourself walking over the words of the person on the other end of the call. Mentally count "1-1000, 2-1000" before responding to their words to be sure they are finished, and not just coming up for air between sentences.

Tone is also hugely important. Think about it: when you call someone, and they answer the phone with a tone that implies you're a major interruption to their normal day, how likely are you to want to call back? It doesn't matter what the purpose or point of the call is; you're predisposed to have a negative reaction. On the other hand, if someone answers in a pleasant or welcoming tone, you're better prepared for a positive discussion.

It's important to remember: you have less than 27 seconds to make a positive first impression on the phone. The reality is, you have about 10-15 seconds to get past the first "keep or put back" decision point when you're dealing with someone over the phone. The other person doesn't have the benefit of seeing part of your overall "package." Words, tone and message are all you have to work with, and your message won't be heard if your tone doesn't work.

Written word

In this age of technology, don't discount the power of the written word. We have always relied on written communications to do business, and make acquaintances, both socially and professionally. But, the way we communicate has changed drastically, particularly since the advent of the Internet.

Now, when we use written words to communicate, we remove another layer of "personal" from our message. Of all the senses we were able to utilize when interacting face-to-face (words, tone, body language, facial expression), we now are down to only one—words. And, if we aren't careful with the words we choose, we can find ourselves missing our goal by miscommunicating our message.

There's one more layer of "personal" we can use with the written word that has all but fallen out of practice—hand-written letters or notes. We all rely so much on computer-generated content that we have all but forgotten how to *write*. However, if you are trying to make a personal connection with someone, think about what would leave a more significant impression: a laser-printed note, or one that is hand-written? I'm not saying we should always hand-write our letters, but there are times where coming back to the personal touch is better.

Think about what it says: most of us write more slowly than we type. When hand-writing a note, we have to take extra care because we can't "erase" or "delete" when using pen and paper. Taking the time and care to hand-write a thank you note, for example, implies a higher level of value or importance: you took the time to do it by hand, and do it right. Your handwriting can even convey part of your personality that you just can't get by using the computer—no matter how many clever "smileys" you use.

When writing anything, however, the most effective correspondence is one that considers the recipient's point of view or area of interest. Unless you are writing a "just catching up" letter to a personal friend, your correspondence is trying to communicate a message.

This means you might want to consider who your audience is, particularly if you are communicating cross-culturally (and I even mean that within the United States, not necessarily international communication). Avoid slang or trendy phrases whenever possible, because you can't assume your recipient is familiar with regional expressions.

Also, make sure the overall tone of your communication is at an appropriate level of formality or informality, even if it's "just a note." And, while this may be obvious to most people, spell-check or proof-read your content carefully before committing to sending it, regardless of what method of delivery you use. Something that is written in a sloppy manner reflects back on you, the author. Again, it's another way to make sure your image is consistently reflected in all you do and are.

WHEN TECHNOLOGY IS **NOT** YOUR FRIEND

Let's be direct here: for most of us, technology has been an enormous blessing. We have the ability to stay in touch, reach out globally, and be continually connected to business, family and friends. We can get content of any sort delivered to us at any time, regardless of where we are. While that is mostly a good thing, there are times where this "on-line, all the time, anywhere" capability can cause problems or interfere with our relationships, both personal and professional. Let's take a look at some of those and examine how "bigger, faster, in more places" isn't always *better*.

One of the amazing benefits of our new, wired world is the ability to multi-task. We can be standing in line at a bank, and still be getting and responding to emails. We can watch a streaming video of an important press conference and send an IM on our phone to alert someone who may have an interest in the proceedings. We get an alert on our cell phone or PDA when someone has replied to an important post we have on the Internet, and we can instantly respond. All this is well and good, except that for many of us this multi-tasking has become a habit that we have difficulty putting aside.

In Chapter Three, we discussed how rude or disruptive it can be when people are answering emails or texting during a meeting. But do you realize that it gets even worse? In my presentations to business leaders, they have shared that they have had job candidates actually texting or answering non-related emails *while in the middle of an interview*! What message do you think that conveys to the prospective employer? It is not only disrespectful and rude, but literally shouts, "What I'm doing is more important than giving you my attention and interest."

Now, it's one thing to take an emergency phone call. (I would hope still that the candidate would excuse him- or herself to take that call, and not have the entire conversation in the interviewer's office.) But to sit there and click-click-click away during an interview…that's not a way to impress a future employer, or at least not in the way you'd like!

Also, many of us have found that our multi-tasking habit can work against us. Carrying on a phone conversation while doing something unrelated to your conversation can become problematic. Even if the caller can't hear you typing or shuffling papers, you can get "lost" in the conversation, or get so wrapped up in what you are reading or writing that you just respond to your caller with an unfocused, "uh, huh…" Again, it conveys the message that you are not really engaged in the conversation, or focusing on the caller.

Cell phone calls are another possible negative. While having a phone with us at all times can be a great convenience, remember that not everyone wants to be part of your conversation. Before answering a call, or initiating one, look around you: is this the right time or place to be having this call?

So many people are completely self-absorbed in their "business" that they are completely oblivious of others around them. Everyone can recite examples of loud, obnoxious callers who drone on and on in a crowded place, talking about the vendor that cheated them, or how Aunt Mabel's liposuction turned out. Really, not all of us need or want to know this.

Please remember to keep your voice down and really take an assessment of where you are and what you are doing before you decide to jump on that phone. Just because you can, doesn't always mean you should. If you go back to the earlier point that you should always assume that someone is watching you, add this to your awareness: they may be listening, too, and you never know who that person is sitting at the adjacent table. It is a very small world.

Summary

While we like to believe that people don't "judge the book by the cover," in truth our brains are programmed to do just that. This is particularly true in business, where image is important, (unless you are a hermit working in a cave producing artisan cheeses). If image wasn't a big deal, there wouldn't be such emphasis on "branding" in the business world.

We need to be conscious of what our image says about us: how we dress, how we speak, how we act. What picture are we painting in the eye of the beholder? Is that consistent with how we want them to see us? It's important to take an honest assessment of how we come across. Imagine you are looking in a mirror: what do you think others see when they look at you, or watch you in action?

There's a lot involved in developing our "image." How we dress. The words we choose, whether in speaking or writing. Even the tone of our voice can play a significant part in influencing the impression we make on a first meeting, and reinforcing or negating that impression in subsequent exposure.

The good news is that there is no right or wrong that applies in every situation. You should, however, always think about the expectations of other people you're interacting with. Sometimes "right" means meeting those expectations, while at other time presenting a different image is more appropriate.

Whatever your goal, realize that *you* are in charge of your packaging. As someone once told me, "To be the somebody you want to be, you have to *be* that somebody."

TAKE ⌛ FIVE

Try these suggestions for making sure the image you present is the one you intend for people to see. Keep in mind that "Perception IS reality."

- ☐ Before your next phone-call, try to put yourself in a positive mindset, or even practice smiling, before you pick up the phone. You may find it makes an enormous difference in the tone—and the outcome—of the call.

- ☐ If practical, move your phone or computer to some place in your office that makes it less easy to multi-task during phone calls. Try to make it a practice to be fully-engaged during your call. Arrange your callbacks for a time when you know you can dedicate yourself to your calls. Try not to cram too much in at once. This may be hard to do because we all are so busy, but you'll find your phone calls are more productive if you focus on the job at hand.

- ☐ Write down the name of the person you are calling, or is calling you, and use their name periodically throughout the call.

- ☐ Before meeting someone in person for the first time, find a mirror in a restroom and check yourself out. What you see is what they see. Straighten the tie, tuck in the shirt, comb your hair, whatever you need to do to look "together." Take a quick gander at the "rear view," too. Many folks neglect to do this…and it can be embarrassingly obvious if you don't.

☐ Wash and wipe your hands completely DRY before you will be shaking hands with someone, particularly if you've just used the washroom. There is nothing worse than shaking a wet or clammy hand!

☐ Practice "eye contact" at every opportunity, so it becomes a habit. Do it at the store, at home with your family, people you pass on the street. Make it second nature so you don't have to think about it when meeting someone new.

chapter Six

SIX SIMPLE WAYS TO BUILD LASTING CONNECTIONS

Although using the techniques and tips I'm about to share with you hardly qualifies as "rocket science," you would be surprised (or maybe NOT when you consider how people treat each other these days) how few people even bother to make the effort. As you read through this, you might think, "Well, a lot of this is just basic common courtesy." But courtesy these days is anything but common. In the highly competitive business world, many people are looking to gain that edge, often at the cost of other people's need or feelings. "It's just business," after all, so anything goes. But, the truth is, the end does not always justify the means.

Consider this: your "means" are an important factor in how you build and develop relationships. In the future, you may need those relationships in ways you might not be able to anticipate right now. "You just never know," is an important consideration and should be a guiding point for your interactions at all times.

Make sure the impression you leave is a good one, as we discussed in the previous chapter. In this chapter, we'll talk about more ways you can ensure that you do just that.

EVALUATE ALL ACTIONS BY THE GOLDEN RULE

It may seem old-fashioned to some, but there is one particular "rule" you can use to guide your actions that will get you through 99.9% of the situations in good shape. Certainly many of you have heard of "The Golden Rule" (and no, it is NOT "He who has the most gold rules"). One basic version states "Treat others the way YOU want them to treat YOU." There's another variation of this often referred to the "Platinum Rule," so called because supposedly it's better than the Golden Rule and it says, "Treat others the way THEY want to be treated." Regardless of which version you pick, the general concept is the same.

Many will point to Judeo-Christian origins of the Golden Rule, and they would be partially correct. It's true that both the Old and New Testaments in the Bible include versions of this statement. But, if you really research the concept you'll see that this "rule" is universal.

The ancient Chinese philosopher Confucius stated, "What you do not wish for yourself, do not do to others." Even earlier, Aristotle advised, "We should behave to others as we wish others to behave to us." Immanuel Kant, 18th century German philosopher, counseled: "Act as if the maxim of thy action were to become by thy will a universal law of nature." Buddha offered, "Hurt not others in ways that you yourself would find hurtful." This is all very good advice.

So you see, what we're talking about is a universal truth. You can't have any community or society, religious or not, that doesn't believe and adhere to some form of the Golden Rule. Without consideration for the needs, feelings and wants of others, you don't have a community; you have anarchy.

Business is no different. While the nature of business may find you in competition or conflict with others, it doesn't mean business operates by different rules. At some point, you have to interact, cooperate, and communicate with others. You'll need those others to get what you need, want and are striving for. Again, as we said before, it's not all about "you."

Keep in mind, when I talk about using the Golden Rule, I don't mean just rolling over and becoming a doormat. You don't unilaterally give up your needs for those of others. But you must consider their point of view or objectives in order to have more successful business relationships.

It's not hard to ask yourself this simple question before you do something, say something or take action: "if it were me, would I like to be treated/spoken to/involved in this way?" It's a great litmus test for your interactions, and even in times of stress or conflict, you can use it to assess better, if not ideal, ways to treat people.

For example, say you have to let an employee go for whatever reason—even possibly because of misconduct. Before you deliver the bad news, you can use the Golden Rule to consider how to let them go with dignity and respect, even if they haven't treated you or your organization the same way.

That brings me to an interesting point: the Golden Rule does not say "Treat others the way they TREAT you." Someone may treat you with disdain, disrespect, or even complete lack of courtesy and decorum. That does not give you license to treat them in-kind.

In fact, you may have more to gain by continuing to treat them decently, in spite of their bad conduct. Consider a tough negotiation, perhaps even a hostile one. It would be completely expected to give as good as you are getting, to be harsh, unrelenting, even rude. Heated negotiations are often very volatile.

But even Sun Tzu, military strategist and author of "The Art of War," believed in the absolute importance of character, that respect and trust had to be earned. Now, imagine that you are in the middle of the hot negotiation, with the other side attempting to resort to intimidation or bullying tactics to make their point or gain advantage. You, on the other hand, refuse to be baited, remaining calm, courteous and respectful. Who do you think *really* has the greater edge?

One of Sun Tzu's famous quotes is "What the ancients called a clever fighter is one who not only wins, but excels in winning with ease." You can't do that if you are reacting from emotion rather than responding with control. The Golden Rule can help you keep your responses reasonable, because you won't abuse your opponent when you, yourself, don't appreciate being abused.

IS IT FAIR TO ALL CONCERNED?

"It is Fair to all concerned," may sound familiar to you, particularly if you are a Rotarian, or know anything about Rotary International. It is the second point in what is referred to as "The Four-Way Test," which is what Rotarians are advised to use when evaluating any interaction. Originally crafted by Herbert J. Taylor, the Four-

Way Test was designed as an "ethical yardstick" for Mr. Taylor's employees. Today, it has become the method for broadly assessing "Of the things we think, say or do…" (this is the preamble to the 4-Way Test).

Considering whether something is fair to the other party is a great foundation for building a lasting business relationship. Trust is vital to the success of business connections. You won't be considered someone worthy of trust if you make a habit of treating people unfairly.

Some ways to put in practice fair treatment might be to offer something to someone else at least as often as you ask for something for yourself. Another practice might be to seriously consider providing fair compensation for a task you require, even if you can get that service for less. For example, in a tough economy, there are people who will do just about anything for incredibly low fees. But you'll be more likely to build trust and loyalty with them if you are fair in what you pay, even if it's more than they ask for.

At this point, you may be telling yourself, "oh, that's all well and good, but we all KNOW life isn't fair." True. Too often, life is not fair. But that doesn't mean you have to be the one who continues to propagate the unfairness of the world. You cannot control the outside world; you can control yourself and how you choose to deal with others.

While you can use unfair tactics and pressure to bend people to your will, you cannot earn their trust using those methods. That requires fairness and decent treatment. Machiavelli may have been a brilliant statesman and schemer, but I can tell you no one trusted him, and he rarely rested peacefully at night.

Certainly, there are people without a conscience who will do anything to get ahead. I don't believe those people are buying and reading this book because they don't care about others, or about their ability to build good relationships. What I'm saying is that if you want to be successful in developing, nurturing and growing effective relationships, you'll have to do it on a basis of trust. That will only occur if you are dependably fair to others.

Your reputation for fairness will also go a long way to insulating you on those rare occasions where something happens that prevents you from being fair. In those cases, inequity is clearly the exception. People will cut you some slack if they know this is not your normal way of doing business.

COURTESY COUNTS: INCLUSIVE LANGUAGE

"Every progressive business man will agree with the successful Western manufacturer who says that 'courtesy can pay larger dividends in proportion to the effort expended than any other of the many human characteristics which might be classed as Instruments of Accomplishment." So goes the opening line in an essay on "The Value of Courtesy" written in the early 1900's. While this phrase may be more than 100 years old, I would say that the sentiment behind it is just as true now as it was then…perhaps even more so when you consider how discourteous our society has become as a rule.

If you doubt the value and impact of simple courtesy, consider this: which are you more likely to open, a mass-distributed email, or one that is clearly individualized and personal? (No, I don't mean using those cool tools that automatically insert the recipient's name in a form letter. It's doubly tacky when the inevitable "glitch" happens and you end up with "Dear Email Recipient" in the header followed by a space later in the body of the letter. It's really obvious your "personal" letter was anything but, particularly when the "To" field is addressed to "undisclosed-recipients.")

Being courteous in business doesn't mean you are "easy" or "wimpy." We aren't talking Little Lord Fauntleroy by any means. When you are courteous in your business dealings, it shows you care about your customers, suppliers, and employees. It shows that you understand how important it is to treat them with consideration. Courteous actions, language, and behaviors are some of the outward ways we demonstrate our underlying consideration and respect.

It's not really hard to be courteous. Most of us were taught to say "Please" and "Thank you" as children. But over time, we've gotten careless, and our use of those "Magic Words" has atrophied. While they seem so basic, it's really amazing to see how infrequently they are used.

It may seem like such a little thing, but the little things go a long way toward developing a more positive and respectful business culture. Being rude (or even merely abrupt) tends to put people on the defensive. When you use courteous words and phrases, you are building bridges between you and another person.

With your choice of words, you indicate respect and care for the other person. It's easy to blow off someone who doesn't matter to us; we take care with people who matter. With courtesy comes *inclusiveness*, rather than excluding or dismissing people.

Here are some simple phrases to illustrate what I mean. The first column represents phrases we've all likely heard (or spoken). The second is a better, inclusive alternative. As you read the list, think about the feeling each response or phrase brings up. I think we'd all agree we'd rather be spoken to in the second way than the first.

Seriously: would you be more likely to do what someone asked you if they used phrases in Column 1, or Column 2?

Again, it may seem like "no big deal," but really, the simple courtesies you extend to others are hugely valuable. If you recall from Chapter Four, we talked about striving to find the mutual-win in any interaction. Operating from a position of courtesy will always fit that goal, because courtesy is a "win" regardless of whether you are on the giving or receiving end.

You are more likely to be treated with respect and courtesy if you lead by positive example. If nothing else, your interactions with others will be more pleasant. If you make this a habit, you may find your overall communication pattern to be more positive and less stressful. You are also likely to be more successful, because you'll be a pleasure to do business with, rather than a pain!

TAKING CREDIT, TAKING RESPONSIBILITY

Speaking of the oft-overlooked "I'm sorry," one of the biggest ills in business today is people's inability to take ownership for their own mistakes. There are too many people in this world who habitually blame others for their problems or, worse, use others or outside factors as scapegoats.

I'm sure we can all think of someone like this: no matter what the issue, there's always someone or something else to blame. There are also individuals who, given a difficult task or mission, strive to find a way to put others on the critical path. That way, they can always point to a lack of follow-through, return correspondence, or something similar as proof that the other party "dropped the ball." How many times have you heard something like this: "Well, I sent them the email…" or "…left them a message," the implication being that someone else let you down, while that person did what you expected them to do.

Nobody likes the person who is always shirking responsibility and dodging blame. Again, if you're trying to build trust and respect in business, this won't do it. We are getting into the area of ethics and integrity here. Taking ownership for your "business"—for good or bad—is a primary factor in being considered ethical.

Nowadays, the "New Integrity" is too often being really, REALLY sorry when you are caught doing wrong–it's not what keeps you from doing wrong in the first place. Face it: we all blow it from time to time. Real character and integrity means owning up to the mistake, taking responsibility, and making things right, as much as is possible.

Another problem that is essentially the other extreme, but equally troubling, is taking credit for things that you didn't do. There are degrees of this issue: referring to a report as "yours" when others have made significant contributions, claiming original authorship for an idea you got from someone or somewhere else, and suggesting that you were the initiator of a unique process or solution when you know it came from another source.

Even a simple, "I've been telling him/her that for weeks," and negating another person's thought or suggestion is a subtle form of claiming responsibility for something that wasn't yours to own. It's normal. Many of us are worried about having our contributions overlooked, so we tend to toot our own horn as much as possible.

If we stop and consider that business isn't a zero-sum game, we will realize that we gain more by including others than shutting them down. When we do that, we find the "mutual-win" once again.

UNDERSTANDING EFFECTIVE COMMUNICATION

I don't mean to oversimplify things, but really, the most effective communication is the kind you, yourself, wouldn't mind receiving. Granted, everyone's "incivility" filter is set somewhat differently. But as a general rule, we do know what considerate language or phrasing is, and what it is not. Answering the phone with, "Yeah, what do you want," probably isn't the best form of customer service, for example. But even if those words aren't used, don't you frequently feel as though that's the attitude or tone behind the words?

Since rudeness and incivility in the workplace is so pervasive, truly kind and considerate communication is a refreshing relief. It can really get you noticed. Since we already know that "like begets like," one effective way of improving the work environment is to lead by positive example.

We're always quick to see when other people are rude or callous towards us, yet we often don't recognize our role in the tenor of the workplace. In a study by the University of North Carolina, more than 1,600 subjects were asked if they thought rudeness, backstabbing, poor communication and general incivility existed in their places of business. While 89% of those respondents agreed with that statement, when they were asked if they were guilty of this kind of behavior in the workplace, 99% of them said no. This isn't the only such study, but I don't think we need to go into them all—you get the picture.

We know how prevalent rude and indifferent behavior is in the business world. We also know that companies that base their dealings on respect, consideration and trust tend to do better, both internally and externally. So the question is, why aren't more people turning back to "good old-fashioned courtesy?"

The answer is that it takes an outward focus, and most people are still thinking about "me, myself, and I" first and foremost. When you adopt an outward-focused approach, and use written and verbal communication that reflects that, you are viewed by others in the organization — whether peers, direct reports, or superiors — as being someone who is a positive influence in the company.

Another thing to consider is the potential permanence of today's communication, particularly when written in any form. Nowadays, you just don't know what is getting stored in email, on servers, or on the Internet. Before you commit anything to writing, think about not only what you are saying, but how you say it, and how it might be interpreted.

Even if you are just making a joke about your boss or someone in another organization, it's possible that your message might be misinterpreted or misused. You'd hate to be in a meeting five years from now, only to find that someone Googled you and discovered something you said that puts you in a very unflattering light — or worse. It really is true: "if you can't say something nice, don't say anything at all," or at least be diplomatic about your comments. You never know who might hear or see them.

This is particularly true of social media and networking sites. We think we have a safe forum in which to "share," but you have to be cautious. Not only of what you say, but of what you share about yourself and others. For example, I've had my Facebook friends share things about themselves that have caused me to completely reevaluate what kind of person they must be.

There are just certain aspects of your life, whether business or personal, that you just shouldn't share in this way. I can tell you, if my contact ever wanted to use me as a reference or ask me for a referral, I would now think twice before doing it, just because of what I learned from Facebook.

Also keep in mind that the more "connections" you have, the more possible exposure points, because you have X number of friends or contacts, and they each have their own list. It's no longer a matter of six degrees of separation — with technology as far-reaching as it is, the number of "degrees" seems to be more like *two*.

Technology has another inherent challenge: when we are emailing, IM-ing, or texting, it's easy to forget that we're dealing with another human on the other end of our keyboard, particularly when people use created or anonymous user id's. When someone makes a comment that is irritating, "snarky," or even rude, our natural instincts kick in and we just want to blast them back. Back in the 1980's, there was even a "protective measure" early Internet and email/forum users put into action, warning people of an impending rant by asking them to "don their flame-protective gear." Meaning, you're about to get vilified; hope you're ready.

So generally, consider this easy test before you say or write anything: "would you be comfortable saying this to the person's face?" Now, some people can be complete jerks and can say anything to someone's face. But for most of us, we can't rip someone to shreds in person. So use the same consideration, whether you are sending an email, talking on the phone, chatting, IM-ing, or communicating in any other way. If you combine this rule with the Golden Rule, you'll do just fine.

Honesty is the best policy, but be careful how honest you are

For many of us, this is an obvious point, but in the quest of trying to be "honest," we sometimes cross the line between "honesty" and "brutality." We talked about honesty and truthfulness earlier in this chapter, but I want to come at it at a different angle, given that we just covered the idea of effective and considerate communication.

While we do want to remain honest in our communications, there are times where it's better to say too little than to say too much. I personally value directness in communication. I like to say, "I'd rather take a bad truth than a good lie." But not everyone is wired that way. We don't want someone to keep the truth from us, but we don't want the truth to hurt, either.

There are many good lines about how "the truth will set us free," and "When in doubt, tell the truth," but sometimes we also have to use our judgment when we're being "truthful." It's also equally true that "the truth hurts." It's our job to be sure we are being diplomatic, saving someone's feelings and dignity, while at the same time being honest.

If you are unclear of the distinction, let me ask you to analyze a question and think about what you believe is the best way to answer. Your best friend, dearest relative, or spouse comes to you with a new outfit and asks, "Does this make me look fat?" Where are you going to go with this "truth?" Perhaps the person asking the question does display a bit of chunk, or appears that way, in said outfit. Hmmm?

One form of the truth could leave both parties feeling satisfied…the other…well, opportunity for swift and certain death, no?

As with all forms of communication we've discussed in this chapter, always put yourself in the position of the receiver: "If it were me, how would I want to hear this?" We're so used to having our leg pulled, or being "B-S'ed," so frequently that we believe hearing the plain, unvarnished truth would be a pleasant change. Just remember that you can be kind, considering the other person's feelings, and at the same time be direct and honest. That's the better way, the one more likely to keep you in a positive light.

SUMMARY

This chapter was all about the actions, words, and underlying thoughts that lead to developing more positive, effective and productive relationships with anyone in the workplace. It really comes down to one main thing: putting yourself in the other person's shoes, and letting that perspective guide all you do and say.

The "little courtesies" do really mean a lot, even today. Especially today, when we have only to look around us briefly to see how rude, crude and indifferent our society has become.

Treating other people with genuine kindness, courtesy and consideration is the best way to leave a positive impression. When you lead by this positive example, you'll be pleased at how much easier your interactions are with others, and how much better your results!

When you remember that we'd all rather work and be around people who value us, it becomes clear why treating others this way is a powerful way to stand out, be noticed, and make a lasting impact.

TAKE ⧖ FIVE

Here are a few quick suggestions for enhancing your abilities to make and grow lasting positive connections:

- ☐ Work on your friendliness quotient with a few simple tasks. For example, if you see someone rushing to the elevator, but the door is closing, find the "door open" button and hold the elevator for them. Smile at the person when they come into the elevator or welcome them "aboard."

- ☐ For some people, making eye contact, much less talking to someone, on an elevator is hugely difficult. Be friendly and outgoing in the elevator, and you'll find it comes much more naturally to you in all sorts of other situations.

- ☐ Make it a practice to give someone a genuine compliment every day. We tend to notice when things aren't going right—make it a habit to look for the good things that people do or who they are and recognize that in them. You may be surprised at the results!

- ☐ Call, email or personally greet one person each day who would not expect to hear from you. Let them know you were thinking of them. Ask if they need assistance with anything, or if you can provide any information that might be beneficial to their work.

- ☐ Pause before acting or responding to any communication you receive that you interpret as negative. Assume the sender is standing in front of you at that moment, and only respond in a manner you would be comfortable saying directly to them.

chapter Seven

SECRET #5:

YOU CAN NEVER SAY THANK YOU TOO EARLY OR TOO OFTEN

When was the last time someone thanked you for something "just because?" It didn't have to be for anything particularly out-of-the-ordinary. In fact, it's likely that the thank you was more notable simply because you didn't do anything heroic to get it.

We naturally expect that in business, we always hear about what was wrong, what didn't go well, or how we failed to meet someone's expectations. THEN we hear about it, and how! But, it's not so typical to hear appreciation. I think part of the reason we have learned to pat ourselves on the back so often is because we don't see anyone else doing it, even when we truly deserve it.

This chapter explains how vital it can be to your relationships and connections to thank people and be appreciative of their efforts, talents, and time. We'll explore several ways you can show gratitude, and how it will come back to reward you in the future.

SHOWING APPRECIATION

As human beings, we all have some basic needs, and one of them is to be recognized for who we are and what we do. We all have a universal desire to feel appreciated. Yet, we often feel as though no one notices the efforts we make or the results we achieve.

In business, this is particularly important. As someone once shared with me, "Money may get them into your company's front door, but appreciation and recognition is what'll keep them from going out the back." While it may seem as though people change jobs for money, surveys repeatedly show that the primary reason people leave is that they feel unappreciated and under-valued.

It's somewhat expected that we don't make showing appreciation a priority. Business is chaotic. We're focused on getting things done, meeting milestones, and finishing projects. We overlook the need to say thanks to those people who have helped us. Is it any wonder that we've had to adopt "Administrative Official's Day" (formerly known by the not-so-Politically-Correct phrase "Secretary's Day") or, in schools, "Teacher Appreciation Week?" We have to make it official, because we've forgotten to do it as a normal course of business.

But appreciation isn't just a tremendous motivator. It can also help forge strong connections, across and beyond organizations. We generally prefer doing things for others when we know they are grateful, and appreciate our efforts. This is true in the personal and social world–it's no less true in business.

Think about it: you're more likely to feel good about staying late to finish a project when your boss praises you, and recognizes your extra effort, right? (Assuming that he or she doesn't make a habit out of calling for this extra effort.) If we feel our efforts are appreciated, when we're called on to do it again, we're more likely to agree.

In our schools-based SocialSmarts program, we call this developing an "Attitude of Gratitude." We talk about how a grateful outlook can lead to many different positive effects. In the media, the news, and in our own daily lives, there is a lot of emphasis on things that we are missing out on, or lacking. Marketing messages continually reinforce the idea that life would be perfect if *only* we had this latest and greatest…whatever it is. Is it any wonder we've forgotten what gratitude is and how to practice it?

When we have an Attitude of Gratitude, we tend to appreciate even the little things more. We realize how many good things really happen to us, and how much we already have in our lives. People who look at life with a glass half full mentality also tend to attract more positive things in their lives. It stands to reason, then, that grateful people tend to appreciate others more, too, and generally express it. This leads to more positive relationships. Do you see how powerful appreciation can be?

Here are a couple of points about showing appreciation and thanking people. First, be sincere. Most people have a highly tuned filter for people who are just heaping on gratuitous praise or comments in an effort to get on someone's good side. Do you recall the scene from the blockbuster movie "Pretty Woman" where the store clerk is dishing out sappy compliment after compliment to Richard Gere? He comments to the clerk, "More sucking up," and then points to Julia Roberts — the real customer — and says, "not to me…her." The point is we quickly know when someone is being genuine, and when they're "sucking up."

Another thing to remember is that even the most sincere praise can become tedious when overused. It's like a special spice — we love to taste a particular flavor in a dish. But even if we love it, the taste quickly gets old or even disappears to our taste buds if we have it day after day. So use praise judiciously and genuinely. That way it continues to be very effective.

THANK OTHERS FOR THE JOURNEY, NOT JUST THE DESTINATION

After reading the previous section, you might tell yourself, "Ok, I can remember to thank my team after the next project is done," or "when we land this partnership." But what about all the little steps and milestones in between? What will you do if you don't succeed in your endeavors? No doubt, there are intermediate stops along the way in which people have expended effort and energy, worked hard for a mutual goal, maybe even gone out of their way to be creative and innovative. All those are opportunities to thank them, recognize their contributions, and communicate their value to you and your organization.

Let me give you an interesting example: my husband is a nationally-recognized charity auctioneer. He often points out to his audiences the value of the second-, third- or fourth- high bidder on any item. As he explains it, while we may *collect* the money from the high-bidder, it's the non-winning but participating bidders that help make the charity more money. They increase the amounts of the bids just by raising their bid cards.

Similarly, I personally swam my fastest time ever in my high school swimming career the day I was assigned to the lane next to the division's fastest competitor. It's the competition, the participation of the others that often encourages the best performance. Recognizing that, and praising or even *rewarding* the contribution is often stronger than recognizing only the winners.

As my husband often says to the second and third highest bidders at the close of a bid, "Thank you for helping us get there. We couldn't have done it without you." You might want to consider how you can incorporate that kind of gratitude into your way of doing business, or interacting with others.

One thing we frequently discount or overlook completely is the value of time. Of all the resources we have at our disposal, time is the only one we can't renew or get back. We have a finite amount of time. Consequently, when someone contributes their time or participates directly in an activity, this is extremely valuable, regardless of the outcome.

Consider what is more personal, and therefore valuable: having someone merely write a check, or seeing someone get personally involved in a project? Anyone can write a check, but not everyone is willing or able to take personal action. When someone gives of themselves, in any capacity, that's a pretty major contribution.

We have a natural tendency to underestimate and, consequently, undervalue the importance of time. That means we must make a point of recognizing and appreciating it when others offer their time and personal involvement. It's so significant that we even incorporated a routine and practice into our children's SocialSmarts curriculum that is meant to call attention, and appreciate, the value of other people's time or interaction.

In SocialSmarts, students are taught that, beyond just saying "good bye" when you leave, you should take it to the next level by adding a "thank you." So, for a child who is getting ready to leave a play date, it's appropriate to say, "Good bye and thank you for having me over." We can use this paradigm in business by adding the thank you as part of our business dealings. Ending a meeting with "thank you for your time" is a simple way to recognize the value of the interaction or opportunity to meet.

You may want to personalize the way you say it so it feels genuine and not cookie-cutter, but you get the general idea. The idea is to recognize the value of the time, participation, and attention of the other people involved, and express gratitude when someone gives of this non-renewable resource.

THANK YOU NOTES—AND GIFTS

Just as thank you notes have fallen out of practice in social circles, so have they in the business world, too. It's too bad, because so many people don't know the true power contained in a simple thank you note.

It used to be standard practice, for example, that you write a personal note to a prospective employer after a job interview. These days, hardly anyone ever does it anymore. This is particularly true for younger job seekers. But if you don't do this, you're missing a major opportunity.

You know that of the potentially dozens or even hundreds of candidates seeking this position, very few of them will write a note of thanks for the interview. Don't you think that this small gesture will stand out? It's one more chance to differentiate yourself from the competition, show your appreciation for the time and the opportunity…and you are making a *personal* connection. You can increase that personal factor, too, if the note is handwritten.

There are so many people and so many things vying for our attention and time. It's tough for anyone or anything to really stand out. If we want to connect with people, we have to use those opportunities to *make those connections.* It sounds simple, but so many of us don't utilize them. It's one of the things you can do to create and maintain what's referred to as "top of mind awareness," which means when someone needs a product, service or resource, you want them to instantly think of YOU.

Let me tell you about the power of a thank you note in business. I'm acquainted with a local orthodontist who has a unique thank you process as part of his business. When the kids have their braces removed, he has them write a thank you note…to their parents.

What impact do you think it has on mom and dad, when a few days after their child has been "de-banded," they receive a note mailed to the home in which the child has written, in their own handwriting and their own words, "Thanks Mom and Dad for getting me braces. My smile is so terrific now!" Wow. When you've gone through a long process and shelled out potentially thousands of dollars to get your kids braces, the impression that leaves on you—both about your child's gratitude and the people who are providing the service—is huge. The next time someone asks you for a referral for an orthodontist, aren't you likely to remember this special treatment, and mention his name?

Gifts can be another great way to make and reinforce connections. When someone has done something nice for you, or even shared something that has left a significant impact, there's nothing wrong with saying thank you in a tangible way. If you know, for example, that your connection enjoys a particular brand of cigars or a fine bottle of wine, you can send that, along with a note, as a token of appreciation.

You may also find an opportunity to send something or give a gift for no particular reason. Say you come across a particular item that seems to be really unique—maybe your business connection collects things along a particular theme, or maybe with a special logo or brand. You happen to find something when you're on a trip and you think of them. Maybe it's a book along the lines of a topic you were both just discussing. It's fine to pick that up and give it to them because you "saw this and it reminded me of you."

Now, let's go back to what we talked about earlier regarding gratuitous thank yous. When we give gifts or send notes, I can't emphasize strongly enough that it must be done out of a genuine feeling of appreciation. And, if you send a gift, it has to be personal. It should also be relatively inexpensive, or it can quickly go from being a token of appreciation to being perceived as a bribe or attempt to influence. Further, if you send something expensive (or send any gifts too often), you stand a chance of embarrassing the recipient or making them feel really uncomfortable. If they begin questioning your motives, the effect of your attempt at connection will be exactly the opposite of what you intended.

Consider also the possibility for the appearance of impropriety or conflict of interest. Some companies have a "no gift" policy, or set a limit at under $50. It goes back to the potential for undue influence or outright bribery, so do be cautious and prudent when sending actual gifts. Even something as well-meaning as a donation to a favorite charity or cause can be perceived as an attempt to influence, so use good judgment. When in doubt, you can always ask about policy.

DO A FRIEND A FAVOR — JUST BECAUSE

Another way we can show our appreciation is by helping others out, when we can. When you have or are building relationships with people, you are interested and concerned with their needs and goals. That's the point of relationship — mutual interest. In the social world, if a friend needed something, or you could lend a hand in some way, you'd probably do it, right? The personal touch in business is no different: your desire is to build a relationship, rather than be seen as a commodity.

It can be something as simple as helping your connection make an introduction with a group or individual you know he or she wants to have or would benefit from. Perhaps you have some data or information they could find useful for a project they are working on. Maybe it's your expertise that you can share, or your experience that can make a job easier. The point is, there's something you have or you can do that would be of assistance and benefit. Sharing is a valuable way to be helpful, be different, and forge those important connections.

It's particularly powerful if you do it without expectations of return. When you do something in the hopes of a reciprocal favor, you're not really offering much. Giving, without expecting to get back, is the purest and best form of gift.

Certainly, we all hope that our generosity isn't merely one-way. We want to know that what we do or give is appreciated. But don't do something for someone else just because you're hoping they'll get the hint and do something for you in return. Again, like gift-giving, your motives will seem suspicious. You will likely irritate or annoy the other person, effectively damaging the connection you were trying to make.

You also need to be careful about the kinds of favors you do. It may be obvious, but it still bears saying that there are certain kinds of things you can do that aren't always appropriate, ethical or even legal. Revealing insider information, for example, no matter how grateful the other party will be if you share, is a really bad idea (as many people in business can attest to, particularly those who have run afoul of the SEC or other authorities).

You also want to be careful about sharing confidential or sensitive relationships. If you're thinking about making introductions to high-powered, celebrity, or other influential people, consider the value and appropriateness of the potential intro from all sides. "What's in it for THEM" from each side's perspective is an important consideration, not just out of respect for the parties involved, but also how it may reflect on you.

So by all means, do others a favor if it's in your power and abilities to do so. But, always operate from a genuine, authentic desire to do good, without expectation of "OK, now you owe me." Also, keep ethics, integrity and appropriateness in mind at all times. You will find giving to be a great way to be personal.

Summary

In this chapter, we discussed many different ways to reconnect with a lost attitude — the Attitude of Gratitude. Being grateful and appreciative can be a huge differentiator these days, when so often the focus is on what's missing, what we don't have, and what we need to have in order to be successful.

Recognizing that others have a significant impact on your abilities to get things done, and complimenting them or thanking them for their contributions is a tremendous way to have a positive, personal touch. If you continue to keep the Golden Rule in mind from our discussions in earlier chapters, you'll quickly see how being appreciative and grateful aligns with an outward-focused way of interacting with others.

There are many ways to show appreciation: a simple compliment or thank you, a hand-written personal note, or even a gift. Always be sure to give your appreciation from the heart. In other words, be genuine about it, or people will tend to suspect your motives, and develop distrust in you personally.

You always want to consider the appropriateness of any tokens of appreciation. Be sure they don't violate any individual or corporate policy. Even the appearance of impropriety is bad, so be smart about what you give, how much, how often and to whom. Used in the right way, appreciation can be a very strong business tool; like a good seasoning, it's great in moderation, and when it fits. Just don't overdue it, or you spoil the whole dish.

TAKE ⏳ FIVE

As you think about how to develop your Attitude of Gratitude, here are a few quick things you can try:

☐ Make it a practice of stopping someone you work with, or who works for you, and thank them for something they've recently done that you haven't recognized in the past. Maybe they've been giving extra effort on a project lately, or came up with a unique solution to a problem. This can be particularly satisfying to the recipient if they feel their contributions haven't been recognized, or that no one else noticed their efforts.

☐ Buy the team coffee "for no reason." Or, if they are snack fiends, maybe go out and get a big basket of candy. Bring donuts in the morning for no particular reason. The point is, think of a little thing you can do that will say thank you, or show them they are valued.

☐ If you can without disrupting critical operations or breaking policy, announce one afternoon, "Ok, everyone's done enough...go home!' If someone has to stay to answer the phones, volunteer to take the duty.

☐ Recognize in public, reprimand in private. Share with all when you praise a team member, share with no one when you must be critical.

chapter Eight

BONUS:

SURVIVING COMMON BUSINESS-SOCIAL SITUATIONS

I n the preceding chapters, we've gone through five important SocialSmarts Secrets you can use to enhance your social capital in business. In this chapter, we are going to look at a few specific situations that tend to be sticking points for many of us.

We're going to cover the basics for some of the most common social situations. We'll go into the details in areas where many people feel challenged, and try to clear up any confusion or uncertainty you may have.

Making conversation

We've all seen it: two people in close proximity. They're supposed to be making conversation–but they discover they have nothing to say to each other. The sound of crickets in the background is practically deafening. The awkwardness is palpable. The worst part is, there's no escape! No one comes to bail them out or rescue them from their inability to converse. We can completely relate to the discomfort of these two individuals, because we've all been there.

Why is this so tough? It's just *talking*, right? We all do it. It's hard, though, when you don't know someone. You can't sense their interests, their personality until they start talking (unless they do something really helpful like wear an entire outfit covered with LA Dodgers logos. There's a good chance that person is a fan!). If you're not blessed with something so simple to use as a hook for starting a conversation, it's up to you to get the ball rolling.

Starting a conversation

Here are some tips you may want to use for starting a conversation, or to keep one going:

- ◆ Try to ask questions of the other person. In general, people like to talk about themselves. You can quickly become known as a great conversationalist, just by knowing how to get others talking.

- ◆ When you ask questions, try to ask open-ended questions; those that can't be answered with a simple yes or no. If you ask closed-ended questions, the conversation can stall. There's nowhere to go with a single-word answer.

- ◆ Typical closed-ended question: "Is this your first time at this Conference?" Same question, but open-ended: "When was the first time you attended this Conference?" And then the follow up: "How has it changed since you first started attending?"

- As a general rule, you may want to avoid some common controversial topics unless you know the specific "commonalities" of others in the room. For example, discussing politics (unless you are asking the other person's opinion only—a good way to learn more about them), money, religion, or gender-specific issues can be dicey.

  Generally safe subjects are movies/entertainment, sports, the stock market in general, weather, books, and music. Other possible good "starter" subjects are food trends, technology, and hobbies. This last one is great! Asking people about what they do in their spare time is a great way to be "personal" in a business setting.

- Spend at least 5 minutes a day checking out the local news or headlines. There's no good reason to not pop onto a "Breaking News" website such as CNN. com to check out what's going on around you.

- If you're traveling, you can also check out the website for the local newspaper. That will give you some idea of what's going on in the area you are visiting. You can use the information you gain to spark a topic of conversation.

  For example, knowing how a popular local sports team is doing can be a great conversation starter—unless, of course, the team is in a major slump. Then, even "Too bad about your Mariners," probably isn't a great way to start out. However, commenting on a specific players' performance or a recent injury, for example, can be a way to reach common ground without emphasizing a disappointing season.

♦ Avoid talking about subjects you aren't familiar with.
If you run into sketchy territory, admit to your lack of
knowledge, rather than trying to bluff your way out of it.
You can actually use your unfamiliarity as a conversation
tool. (For example, "Actually, I just happened to see
something about that in the paper, but I don't really know
much about the issue. Can you fill me in some more?")

Once you've gotten the opening of the conversation out of the
way, you'll need to know how to keep it going. One technique
I recommend is to listen for key words or phrases. These are words
or phrases that you can use in order to ask a follow-up question, or
to move to another topic to chat about.

The goal is to search for common topics that you can use to continue
a dialog. For example, you opened the conversation by asking your
partner how he came to be at this conference. In his answer, he
happens to mention he's from South Carolina. You might pick up
on "South Carolina" and share that you've had a great experience in
Charleston during a business trip, or had the luck to be able to play
in a golf tournament at Hilton Head on vacation. Perhaps you enjoy
Low Country food, or, if you've never tried it, you can ask about
the best places to eat authentic Southern food. Perhaps the Carolina
Panthers are having a great season, or a recent hurricane just barely
missed the state.

Do you get the idea? You have a number of options for discussion,
just by keying in on, and exploring, "South Carolina" when you heard
it in the answer. When you connect via these conversational topics,
you are establishing common ground. This is vital to moving from

strangers to business acquaintances, and then on to possible strategic partners. Now, not every conversation is going to go this way, but you'll certainly never make it to "strategic partner" without one!

Another point: since people *do* like to talk about themselves, be aware of how much time you spending sharing about yourself. One good rule of thumb I use is to ask two questions of the other person for each one I answer about myself. That way I can avoid becoming a crashing bore by monopolizing the conversation.

Ironically, one of the best ways to become known as a great conversationalist is to be a great listener. People will enjoy talking with you. Plus, you'll be surprised how much you learn about them that may be valuable as you work toward furthering relationships, providing better service, and becoming a better businessperson.

INTRODUCING OTHERS

In Chapter Five, we talked about what you do when you meet someone for the first time, in the context of making a first impression. In that section, we touched on the process of "meeting and greeting," including proper handshakes. Recall that, we were focused on one-on-one interactions, in which you introduce yourself. There also will certainly be times where you are called upon to make introductions for others.

There is generally some confusion in these cases: no one seems to be completely sure of the right way to do it: who gets introduced first, what you should say, etc. It's actually much easier to remember this than you may think. Not only can you quickly learn how to do a proper introduction, but I'll also share with you an easy technique you can put into practice that'll take your introductions to the next level.

There are many traditional rules for how to properly introduce people — who's higher ranked, male vs. female first, etc. But, in business, it really comes down to this:

The highest-ranking person is introduced to everyone else first, and those generally in "highest to lowest" ranking order. However, let's be practical: if there are a group of people standing close to each other who are not lined up in rank order, introduce them by who is closest to the highest-ranking person. So, if you're introducing a colleague to the president of XYZ Company, you'd say "Mr. Klein, I'd like you to meet Ms. Diana Cooper, President of XYZ." Then, you'd say to Ms. Cooper, "I'd like you to meet Ron Klein, one of our local associates." Easy, right?

The only exception to this order is this: if you're dealing with a client, the client is always introduced first.

Now, that you have the basics down for the introduction, here's where you can go to the next level. Since these two (or more) people don't know each other, but you do, you can help them find quick common ground by what you say next. In the previous example, when you are introducing your colleague to the company president, you can give them both what I call "magic glue" to help them get a conversation started.

Say, for example, you happen to know that both your colleague and the company president are fans of a particular sports team, or maybe share an alma mater. Use that in your introduction to help connect these two individuals. "Mr. Klein, I'd like you to meet Ms. Diana Cooper...Ms. Cooper, meet Ron Klein. Ron, Ms. Cooper happens to be one of the Patriots' biggest fans and her dad played with them in 1965; I know how much you follow their season."

You can also insert a business context for discussion. For example, let's say your Mr. Klein holds a patent in a particular technology Ms. Cooper's company deals in, or Ms. Cooper recently received an award or other recognition in an area, or for a group, Mr. Klein is familiar with. The idea is to not only make the introduction, but give each party someplace to go other than the standard, "It's nice to meet you." Help them get a bit more comfortable. Make it easy to start a conversation by tossing out the first topic, preferably one in which they share a common interest or awareness.

Another good idea when making introductions is to explain the purpose of arranging the meeting, if it wasn't a purely coincidental meeting. Say something like, "Ms. Cooper, I'd wanted to introduce you to Ron Klein because I think the projects he's been working on at ABC Corporation might be of interest to you at XYZ."

Again, the idea is to offer up some common ground which explains why they might be interested in getting to know each other. Since you are the one arranging and making the introduction, it's your job to help "glue" them together. Then, you've done your job, and it's up to them to continue. Naturally, you're welcome to stay throughout the conversation, as appropriate. But your official job as "introducer" is done. You can graciously leave at this point if you have something else to do, or somewhere else to be.

What do you do if you forget someone's name? Heck, I'm in the business of social skills. I am meeting people all the time. That's a blessing and a curse: I meet so many people on such a frequent basis, that even with the best memory tricks, I forget people's names sometimes. It's not a major crime, so don't stress over it.

If you momentarily forgot someone's name, just admit it. You can even use your embarrassment as a way to ease into re-asking: "You know, I can't believe this has happened to me…I must be losing my mind, but I've just blanked out on your name entirely. " The other person will no doubt say something in an understanding way as he or she repeats the name. "Of course, Damon, I am so sorry… Damon, I'd like to introduce you to Hannah Miller…" It's really only a big deal if you make it a big deal, so go easy on yourself. The moment will pass.

One word of caution: this "forgetting" technique is one that people use sometimes when they want to seem more connected than they really are. Has this ever happened to you: someone *swears* you have both met previously, and this person then goes to great lengths to try to figure out how you already know each other?

They could be genuinely mistaken, or you may have forgotten, so give them the benefit of a doubt. But there are times where you know it's just a ploy to get you to open up or admit a pre-existing acquaintance. Tip: be genuine — if you don't know someone, don't try to fake it. Don't try to sell your way into their circle.

Business Dining

Sharing a meal in a business setting is a common practice, but it's interesting to see how many people don't have a grasp of — or forget/ fail to use — even *basic* dining skills. And, by basic, I mean really basic. Most business meals are not full, formal affairs. They are average, ordinary meals served in a restaurant setting. Yet, even this relatively simple venue and situation requires basic civility, which is too often lacking. So let's do a quick review of a few essential points, just to make certain your next business meal is a success.

While it may seem obvious to many, the proper place for your napkin is in your lap. It's not supposed to be tucked into your shirt collar — that is called a bib, and if your meal requires one (i.e., eating lobster or other shellfish), your waitstaff will likely be prepared with one. If your meal is potentially so messy that you are afraid you'll splatter without "bibbing" yourself up, well, my suggestion is that you order something different.

Practically speaking, if dabbing marinara out of your white shirt or blouse is going to be a problem, save yourself the trouble and stress: order something more manageable. The purpose of having a meeting during a meal is first to have a meeting, with the meal being a secondary priority. Messy meals don't usually combine well with sharp business.

So, rule number one: napkin goes in your lap, preferably as soon as, or shortly after you are seated. This should not be tough to remember. But if it helps, you may make use of the rhyme we use in SocialSmarts for our youngest students (and which I shared with 4 million viewers on *The Today Show*, at the urging of the host): "Clap, clap, clap. Napkin in your lap."

This is particularly effective and memorable when done with the accompanying hand motions, but I don't recommend reciting it during your business lunch!

When you get up from the table temporarily, such as to use the restroom, or to make/take a call, the napkin goes in your chair, not back on the table. When you are finished with the meal, do not throw the napkin in the middle of your plate, regardless of whether the napkin is made of paper or cloth. Retrieving a napkin out of the middle of a meal plate is just plain icky.

When you are finished with your meal, place the napkin, loosely folded, to the left of your plate, or the place setting if your plate has been removed. Also, during your meal, use your napkin to keep your mouth clean — food smears around your mouth or on the drinking glasses are also distracting and uncivilized. Feel free to use the napkin for its intended purpose.

(**Bonus trivia**: did you know the purpose of the napkin is not to keep food off your lap? It's actually there for you to wipe your mouth. If you are eating properly over your plate, any food that drops should, realistically, end up on your plate again, not on your lap.)

When to Start Eating

At a meal served at table, it's proper to wait until everyone has their meal before you begin eating yours. The exceptions would be if it's a multi-course meal and you have ordered a salad, but your dining companion hasn't. While it is implied that you may begin your meal when it's served to you, it's still good courtesy to ask, "Do you mind if I start?" before beginning to eat. That's a sign of respect and consideration for the other person.

If you are eating from a buffet, if there are several diners in the group you may begin when you sit down. If you're with only one or two others, it would be courteous to wait for them to rejoin you at table before you begin eating.

Use of Knife and Fork

No, this is not the place where I discuss the relative merits and sophistication of American vs. Continental style of wielding your knife and fork. (Although I would be more than happy to discuss that with you at any time.) What I will say is this: it's a spoon, not a shovel. Watching some people eat, you'd swear they believe their tool of choice is either a pitchfork or specially-crafted wedge meant for bludgeoning the food into submission.

I have literally seen an adult use one hand to hold his fork, and the other to support the overflowing mass of salad as he pushed it into his mouth. For him, I believe the purpose of the fork was to ensure one hand remained clean during the meal in case he had to shake hands afterwards.

Generally speaking, the purpose of the fork is to humanely spear a small bite and convey it into your mouth. If you don't have an appropriately small piece of food to spear, by all means use that other tool they've given you (the knife!) to turn a larger piece of food into something appropriately small to spear! You do not take a large piece of steak, chicken or vegetable, on the point of your fork and bite a piece off.

Likewise, you don't take said meat or vegetable and, pressing down on your fork with all your might, attempt to fracture off a suitable piece. You have a knife…please do us all a favor and use it! There's nothing more distracting than poor table manners, particularly when you are also trying to impress someone with your business savvy.

Speaking of utensils and napkins…the two should never meet. When you are not using your knife or fork, you place them on the edge of your plate, not on the napkin (and, if the napkin is in your lap where it belongs, you wouldn't be resting your utensils on them anyway, right?)

At the end of the meal, to signal to your waitstaff that you are done with your plate, put your knife and fork parallel to each other diagonally across your plate. The handles should be roughly at a position equal to four o'clock (if you were looking at a clock face) and the points of knife and fork at roughly ten o'clock. The knife is above the fork, with the cutting surface of the knife facing the fork. That's what we call "Done" position in SocialSmarts.

If you are only resting, the knife and fork are crossed across the plate in a rough "X" in front of you, fork over knife, tines of the fork facing down on the plate. To remember that, think of the "No" diagonal line across the sign for "No Parking." The "X" of the fork and knife signify "Not Done."

Finger Food — Yes and No

When I originally joined my first Rotary Club — we met for breakfasts — several of my fellow club members were worried once they found out what I do. You see, I'm one of those people who eat their bacon with fork and knife…and seeing that freaks some people out. They're not sure, you see, what's really considered finger food and what isn't.

Again, much of what is correct, and what isn't, depends on where you are (we can discuss American vs. Continental styles any time…). American table manners generally allow for much greater latitude regarding what you can touch with your fingers during a meal in comparison to other dining styles. I'm not saying it's good or bad here. I'm just describing reality.

Also, there are some conventions that, while proper, aren't obvious. French fries, in a restaurant, are not really supposed to be finger food. Yet, asparagus, as long as it's not smothered in sauce or over-cooked, technically can be. Still, I wouldn't eat asparagus with my fingers in a restaurant. Bacon, likewise, is not really finger food. Fried chicken or ribs is generally OK with fingers, except if you are in an upscale restaurant, in which case you'd eat as much as you could with a knife and fork.

Frankly, in a business situation, I would tend to advise you to choose your selection of food in keeping with the purpose of the meal. If it's casual at a crab shop, for example, then certainly dive in there with the eating utensils you were provided at birth...your fingers. But if you're in a restaurant, that sets the tone for the meal.

Talking While Eating

It can be very tough sometimes to mix business with dining, especially if you are on a tight schedule. Let's face it: chewing food is time-consuming. It can be very tempting to increase meeting efficiency by eating and talking at the same time. But it's terrible to watch and sometimes very difficult to execute, in addition to being poor manners.

How can you talk and chew food simultaneously, without your sentence coming out all garbled? Or, worse yet, without having food coming out of your mouth? Yes, I know we can get very good at tucking our meal into our cheeks like some famished hamster and doing the oral gymnastics required to keep it in place while we talk on. But I can't tell you how little I enjoy seeing my companion's main course being ground into mush, while they explain the value proposition of a business transaction.

If you don't believe me, video tape yourself doing it, or eat in front of a mirror while talking out loud. It's not pretty! I don't know that many of us can carry it off. None of us should attempt to. Even if you try to block your mouth with your hand, it looks Neanderthal. Some people even get their utensils into the act for extra emphasis!

Sometimes, someone will ask you a question, and catch you mid-chew. If this happens, simply raise one finger politely in the universal, "just one moment" sign. They'll get that you are trying to finish your bite. Finish chewing, swallow, make sure your mouth is empty, and then you can respond. No question is so pressing that it cannot wait until you have finished your mouthful.

Oral Hygiene at the table

Yes, I have to write about this. Please, please, please resist the urge to pick/clean/scrape your teeth or gums at the table. I know you're thinking this is so basic, we don't need to talk about it. But we do. I can't tell you how many times you'll see someone picking something nasty out of the molar at the furthest reach of his or her mouth at table. They will even try to be discrete about it, thinking that if they do it behind their hand, no one will notice. But seriously...you can't be subtle about this.

If you have something stuck in your teeth, do everyone a favor. Excuse yourself from the table, and take it off-line to the men's or ladies' room. It's also noticeable when you try to poke around with your tongue, particularly when you are supposed to be having a discussion with someone else. They are looking at you when they're speaking to you; what do you suppose it looks like when your mouth is making contortions like you're the second coming of Jim Carrey?

I don't care if you use a tooth pick, your fork tine, your fingers–you shouldn't do it at the table, no matter how or when. Get that chunk of spinach out from between your teeth in a place more suitable for personal hygiene, please?

There really is enough to talk about in the area of dining and table manners that it deserves its own chapter. The good news is that you can always explore more advanced dining and table manners courses. Not only do you get upper-level dining etiquette, but you also frequently get a great meal out of it, too.

If you're lucky, you might meet other like-minded individuals who also are looking to improve their social skills. These people are also likely to be business folks, so there's much to be gained. Hopefully, this brief section has given you a quick refresher on some common dining do's and don'ts that, while seeming basic, are frequently overlooked. Keep these in mind, and you will come through your next business meal in noticeable style.

COMPANY/BUSINESS PARTIES

One area in which social and business can become a dangerous mix is during a company or office party. Many people forget that, while it is meant to be a social situation, it is still within the context of business. We've all heard stories of the intoxicated employee who takes a photo-copy of his hindquarters during the office celebration. But there are many less-obvious ways to go wrong when business and social are mixed in a party scenario.

The first rule of office-party engagement is that you must remember, at all times and in all circumstances, that it's a business function. When it comes to what you do or say, don't do anything during an office party that you wouldn't do during the normal course of business, even if you are not on the clock. This includes telling inappropriate jokes, making advances on other staff members, gossiping about higher-ups or co-workers, revealing secrets or information meant to be confidential.

I can guarantee you that what happens in Vegas will *not* stay in Vegas if "Vegas" is the office party. What you do in this kind of situation will reflect on your image and performance as an employee. It may even affect your credibility or authority as a leader, and effectiveness as a team player. Keep in mind that no matter what you do, someone may be watching or overhearing you. If you wouldn't say it/do it/ share it openly in the course of a normal business day, don't go there under the misguided belief that the company party is safe.

This is especially important if alcohol is being served. If you are going to drink, be careful and prudent–and not only because you may have to drive afterwards. Many companies are actually avoiding serving alcohol at events these days because of concerns over liability.

But even if you're not driving, alcohol at company functions can be problematic. You may be drinking responsibly, but does someone have the perception that you're overdoing it? You may not feel it, but those drinks may make you more relaxed and less aware of your surroundings. In addition, even though you may be sticking to non-alcoholic choices, if you are in a group that's been drinking, and they get careless with their words or actions, how does that reflect on you? The point is, there are all sorts of potential pitfalls in this scenario, as the following extreme example will share.

I once was hired, for an executive-level position for a nationally-known software products and services company. The day they made the offer, I was called in to the senior exec's office, where he shared with me that I'd now be coming to the position with a new challenge.

Apparently, just the day before, the company had held its annual summer picnic. It seems that many of my would-be team had a problem with their current management, and it all boiled over at the party. Since the company was providing an open bar, several of the employees seriously over-imbibed. Never was the motto "in vino veritas" more true. Inter-employee gossiping led to open hostility and complete loss-of-control, with the bottom line being that all but two of the original 25 employees were summarily dismissed the next day.

I was about to become the executive in charge of a mission-critical software product that no longer had a team to develop it—all because they lost their cool at a company event. They forgot that there is a time and a place to vent your grievances, and the company picnic was neither the time nor the place. (And, in case you're wondering, I did take the job. If the original team was that hostile toward the senior execs, putting a new direct-report exec in the middle wasn't going to rehabilitate the problem. Starting over was the only option. But it remains a great lesson in what *not* to do.)

At this point, it may come to mind that it's safer to just avoid attending a business/social function, rather than to deal with all this hassle. But even that decision can make or cripple your career. Deciding to pass on an invitation to attend could be interpreted as elitism, or proof of your unwillingness to be part of the group. If you have a legitimate conflict, that's fine. But being labeled as a consistent no-show can have a negative effect on your image.

It's important to be an active participant in the business environment. For many organizations, being able to be social in a business context is valuable. It shows you can handle yourself as a positive representative of the company in a variety of circumstances. That's what makes an effective leader. It can be the difference between the corner office and a lifetime in a cubicle.

RECREATIONAL EVENTS

There are many occasions where sports or recreation is combined with business. Similar to the office or company party scenario discussed in the previous section, you want to be cautious about your conduct at special events or occasions.

Again, I can't stress this enough. Whether you are attending a sports event in the company box, playing golf with clients or vendors, or sailing with a small group of business associates and spouses, it's still a business event. It's tempting to just relax and be completely casual, just going with the flow. But if there are business folks involved, it's still a business event. Behave accordingly.

A word of advice: it's tempting sometimes to use extended social events as an opportunity for extended business. Resist the urge to turn a round of golf, for example, into a 4-hour outdoor meeting. As the saying goes, in the first 6 holes you get acquainted, in the next 6 holes you become friends, and the final 6 is when you find areas of mutual interest.

You may have someone's attention and ear in an exclusive way when you are attending an event together. That does not mean you should leverage that opportunity for continual business. That's not the fastest way to get a business connection; it's the fastest way to ensure you won't get a repeat invitation.

If you are there at someone's invitation, let them be the ones to direct the flow of the day. If you are the one extending the invitation, you have more control over when and where to talk shop. Again, don't make business the only, or even the majority, of the conversation. It will seem as though the only reason you extended the invitation was to maneuver your contact into a captive position, plying them with recreation and refreshments. It will seem manipulative even if you didn't mean it to be.

The best business-social situations are where there's an equal balance of both business and fun. If you're going to err on one side or the other, allow it to swing more to fun and social, with business in the background. You'll find it easier to get repeat invitations, and the relationships will be smoother and less forced. When you learn to effectively combine business with social and recreational events, you'll find that each enhances the other.

Summary

This chapter was all about drilling down into some specific scenarios that can either make or break your professional image and your ability to connect with others. Many of these situations cross over between business and social, which is one of the reasons they can be tricky. It's not always easy to remember what is appropriate in a particular situation, especially if the situation appears to be more social than business-focused. It's specifically in those kinds of situations that many people stumble.

Whether you are out at a business meal, company party, or sporting event with business associates, remember that your image can be positively reinforced—or undermined–by what you say and do. Effective business leaders need to be socially adept and comfortable in a myriad of situations. Be sure you're using your SocialSmarts at all times. Avoid common pitfalls by being aware and knowledgeable about what to do…and what not to do.

TAKE ⧖ FIVE

Practice your business-social savvy and fine-tune your abilities to shine in these oft-challenging situations by following these suggestions:

- ☐ The next time you are at a function or event, make it a point of seeking out and meeting someone you don't know, or someone you see standing by him- or herself. Be the first to start the conversation and see how long you can keep it going. Listen for key words you can use to develop your dialog with the other person.

- ☐ Scan the local paper or a news website for some current events. Write down three opening lines you can use to start a conversation. You can make them all generic, or create one specifically for each gender, and one you can use with either gender.

- ☐ Invite a client or colleague out for a round of golf, to a ball game, or other recreational event. Focus exclusively of learning more about that person as a person, not about their business or responsibility. Set the example for them that a social situation with you does not have to be 100% business. This will build trust and comfort for you both, opening the door to a better business relationship when required.

chapter Nine

GOING BEYOND
THE BASICS

There's no way a short book can cover the myriad situations and scenarios in which positive social skills can be used. In fact, I would argue that it's more important to know the foundations for positive social skills than it is to remember all the rules. You can't possibly learn all the rules for all the possibilities, but if you remember the Golden Rule, you'll have a great basis from which to operate.

In any case, you may find that this book has spurred an interest for learning more. You certainly wouldn't be alone. The growth of the personal improvement training field has grown by amazing proportions over the past decade or so. The fastest growing segments in this area have involved personal presentation, business and social etiquette, and international protocol, but these are hardly the only areas you can pursue.

There are classes and books, courses and personal coaching, webinars and systems—the list of resources is nearly endless. Below are some of the options you can investigate, but it's hardly intended to be exhaustive; merely a resource to get you started if you choose to learn more.

BOOKS

Letitia Baldrige's New Complete Guide to Executive Manners,
by Letitia Baldrige

This book provides business leaders and executives practical tips for behavior in business situations. Baldrige discusses not only traditional etiquette rules about such topics as making introductions and using proper forms of address, but it also provides guidelines for other types of behavior, such as dressing appropriately and planning a meeting. This book offers a comprehensive handbook on business manners, combining protocol with common sense.

Netiquette,
by Virgina Shea

Virgina Shea covers a range of "electronic" based rules of conduct in her book, including email, tone and manner in electronic communication, legal and moral issues, and more.

Power Etiquette: What You Don't Know Can Kill Your Career,
by Dana-May Casperson

Can table manners make or break a mega-merger? Can a faxing faux-pas derail a promising business relationship? Can an improper introduction cost you a client? Can manners (or lack of them) really kill a career? Absolutely. In an era when companies are competing on the basis of service, manners are much more than a social nicety—they're a crucial business skill. In fact, good manners are good business. (Source: Amazon.com)

Professional Business Development

Business development coaches usually approach the issue of interpersonal skills from the perspective of the company—what companies can do to build successful leaders, and help companies be more successful. Professional business development coaches often assist in developing strong teams and working on strategy for building effective businesses. That means some aspects of what we've covered in this book about making, keeping and growing strong business connections would certainly be covered by business coaches. But it would be covered from the perspective of the company, not necessarily the individual.

Personal/Professional Coaching

There are any number of sources for this type of specialized training. Whether you are looking for a "certified" coach that can help you with specific areas of etiquette or protocol, or experts in the area of multi-cultural business, you can find someone to help you.

I would strongly recommend that you look for experts that provide what I call "full-spectrum" coaching; that is, ones that give you foundations and "whys" for particular approaches or learning, not just the behavior/action skills themselves. You'll find it easier to extend your learning to new areas if you have a good basis for the behaviors, instead of just relying on specific actions.

I provide this type of coaching, for both individuals and groups. When I consult with clients, I design a program that fits their specific goals. We'll not only cover the basics to ensure you have a solid foundation of skills, but also work on a detailed plan focused on getting you from where you are to where you want to be. Thanks to technology, we have the ability to do this coaching one-on-one, face-to-face regardless of where you might be based, and in what time zone you reside or work.

Introducing Social Skills to Our Youth

Of course, it isn't just the adult professional that can benefit from having excellent social skills. Children benefit, too, as do those around them, when they learn the basics of how to meet and greet, how to conduct themselves around adults and their school-mates, and why it is important to listen more than talk in schools and group environments.

Remember, today's children are tomorrow's business leaders, so if you have a child in your life, get them started early on building a firm social skills foundation. The immediate payback is a happier child, greater success for them in the near term at school and in their relationships, and ultimately, a greater chance at success later in life.

Children's social skills is a topic with which I am very familiar. I am the founder of The PoliteChild, Inc., creator of the SocialSmarts curriculum, which is taught in elementary, middle school and high schools. Many of the social skills I discuss in this book are adapted from my SocialSmarts program. The way I see it, if we can improve the social skills of our youth, then the same principles stand a chance of working for adults!

Summary

While the saying goes, "You can never been too rich or too thin," I would also argue that you can never be too socially savvy. Even when you have a good handle on the basics, there's always room to improve. Because social conventions change, and frankly, situations are always developing that require new policies, rules or best practices, there'll always be new things to learn.

I strongly encourage you to consider the lifetime development of your social capitol to be at least as important as other areas of personal or professional development. This chapter has attempted to give you an idea of the categories of assistance, or sources for development, that exist. Because it's impossible for anyone to review or investigate all of them, I've avoided recommending any specifics.

Before investing in any course or professional coaching, I strongly suggest you ask for references to be sure you're not only getting a good value, but that the product or service you are buying is directed to your specific goals or needs.

Take ⏳ Five

Developing or improving your social skills should be a lifetime goal and process. You have many different avenues you can pursue, but before you invest in any of them, I would suggest the following exercises:

- ☐ Make a list of the areas in which you'd like to improve or learn more. The possibilities for development are literally limitless.

- ☐ Once you've made that list, indicate whether that area is for personal interest, for professional improvement/ development, or both. That should help you prioritize. Before investing in any program or service, go back to your list and see how the offering aligns with your objectives so you are sure you're heading in the direction you want.

- ☐ Every six months, update your list. You'll be surprised how much you'll learn and how much you'll grow. Just being aware of the importance of social capitol for your professional and personal growth will be a strong influencer for absorbing new learning in ways you couldn't predict even six months prior.

Corinne Gregory's

SPEAKING TOPICS

To book Corinne on any of these topics, please call 425.485.4089.
For more information, you may also visit
www.corinnegregory.com or www.socialsmarts.com.

PRESENTATIONS FOR BUSINESS
"Essential SocialSmarts® for Business Leaders"
Society and business are becoming increasingly globalized and diverse. What are the essential interpersonal and communication skills today's leaders need to know in order to stand out from the crowd, and navigate tricky situations?

"Leveraging the Power of Respect"
A presentation for business executives and others in leadership who want to build more creative, innovative teams and business models. Studies show that businesses with cultures based on civility and respect are more productive, innovative, and creative. What are the important traits — for leaders AND teams — and how do you get there?

"CoPowerment®: The Art of Turning 'Me' into 'We'"

After decades of "It's all about ME," "He Who Dies with the Most Toys Wins," and "What's in it for ME," why are some companies faring better than others? As we enter an era where the youngest workers are challenged by a "Me-centric" approach, how do we build successful teams out of a group of independent-minded individuals?

"Overcoming Failure to Educate"

This presentation is appropriate for business leaders, the general public, and anyone concerned about the condition of our public education system. The presentation reveals the many ways in which our educational system is failing our children, and the common underlying thread of failure. It describes the changes that are needed, not only to adequately prepare our youth for their immediate academic success, but even more importantly, for the job market beyond school.

PRESENTATIONS FOR EDUCATORS & ADMINISTRATORS

"7 Steps to Eliminating Bullying in Schools:
An Inside-Out Approach" *(select presentations for Elementary/Primary or Middle/High School)*

Did you know that every year, we spend billions of dollars on anti-bullying programs and initiatives? Find out why traditional approaches aren't working and how you can create a school culture built on respect, compassion, and consideration.

"The Effective Classroom:
How Social Skills Education Improves Academic Outcomes"

What is the biggest obstacle to a truly effective classroom? How do we create optimal learning environments, even at a time where budgets, staffing, and other resources are scarce? Corinne Gregory analyzes the root cause of nearly every problem plaguing our education system today. She shares proven approaches for dealing with them, efficiently and realistically, allowing us to accomplish more, even in a climate of "less."

"The Missing 'Rs:'
Why Reading, 'Riting, and 'Rithmetic are not Enough"
Too many of our students come into school ill-equipped to succeed in the classroom environment, and their social-emotional abilities generally don't improve over time. Learn why the biggest factor in their — and YOUR — success has little to do with academics, yet has EVERYTHING to do with academics.

PRESENTATIONS FOR STUDENTS & YOUTH

"Street Smarts...or SocialSmarts® for Success" *(select presentations for Elementary/Primary, Middle/High School, or College Students)*
Perfect for school assemblies and group meetings!! Students learn why they should care about their social skills and abilities. They discover why good social skills are as important to their success as academics, and make everything else in life come much more easily to them. This presentation is tailored to the age group of the audience, in order to connect with students and make it relevant and interesting. Always a fun talk, whether for 20 or 2000. Even the grown-ups are sure to learn something new and be entertained!

"How Rude!!"
Designed for Teens and Preteens, this 40-minute romp is sure to entertain as it puts a humorous spin on common rude behaviors typically exhibited by kids in this age group. Kids get a kick out of seeing mannerisms and habits they have seen in their friends played

out by an adult — and one that supposedly TEACHES manners and etiquette. The relevance of good social skills and manners is taught by bad example, by being the living image of "what not to do" and then examining the better, positive alternative.

To book Corinne on any of these topics, please call 425.485.4089. For more information, you may also visit www.corinnegregory.com or www.socialsmarts.com.

www.ingramcontent.com/pod-product-compliance
Lightning Source LLC
Chambersburg PA
CBHW060615200326
41521CB00007B/776